# PRAISE FOR
# THE PURPOSE PLAYBOOK

"I know through personal experience how important it is to find resources like *The Purpose Playbook*. The guidance and insights that Alexandra provides throughout the book are invaluable and will undoubtedly help you unlock your potential and leave a positive impact on the world."

– PORTER BRASWELL, CEO of Jopwell
and author of *Let Them See You*

"An approachable, down-to-earth guide for anyone looking to jump toward more fulfilling work, and perhaps in the process, a more purpose-driven life."

– MIKE LEWIS, author of
*When to Jump: If the Job You
Have Isn't the Life You Want*

"Purpose has always seemed so vague. What does it really mean to live on purpose? Cole's analytical mind and articulate writing give readers a realistic roadmap to finding purpose and living with intention. This is a beautiful book filled with actionable steps to help us all come alive."

– KIM LEAR, founder of Inlay Insights
and generational research expert

"If you've been swimming in the deceptively warm waters of your comfort zone for too long or suffering the pain of jamming your heart and soul into a life far too small, this book is for you. Alexandra Cole helps us bust out of limiting beliefs and patterns to reveal the brightest unquenchable fire inside us: our life's purpose."

– BRIDGET FONGER, author of *Superhero of Love: Heal Your Broken Heart & Then Go Save the World*

# THE PURPOSE PLAYBOOK

# THE
# PURPOSE
# PLAYBOOK

## DESIGN YOUR LIFE
## AROUND WHAT MATTERS MOST

### ALEXANDRA COLE

Minneapolis

ISBN 13: 978-1-63489-327-5

Library of Congress Catalog Number: 2020904233
Printed in the United States of America
First Printing: 2020

24  23  22  21  20          5   4   3   2   1

Cover design by Luke Bird
Interior design by Patrick Maloney


Wise Ink Creative Publishing
807 Broadway St NE
Suite 46
Minneapolis, MN, 55413

To order, visit www.itascabooks.com or call 1-800-901-3480.
 Reseller discounts available.

I dedicate this book to my mom, Ingy, who taught me that it is not the number of years you live that matters, but *how* you choose to live them.

# CONTENTS

## PART THREE: LIVE ON PURPOSE

# AUTHOR'S NOTE

To live on purpose is to live in alignment with who you are *destined* to be.

When you are living on purpose, you are pursuing the work, people, and activities that set your soul on fire. You are not beholden to guilt, fear, or shame. You are not concerned with what you *should* be, say, or do. You have a clear understanding of who you are and how you can make an impact by sharing your unique gifts with others. You are unapologetically and wholeheartedly yourself.

That is my wish for you, dear reader.

—Alexandra

# PART ONE

# WHAT IS PURPOSE ANYWAY

> "Do not ask what the world needs. Ask yourself what makes you come alive, because what the world needs is people who have come alive."
> —Howard Thurman

# *PRELUDE*

Have you ever purchased an item of clothing or a pair of shoes that was too small for you? And I don't mean accidentally. I mean you were fully aware that the item was not the right size, but you bought it anyway.

Well, I have. Now, before you judge me for an admittedly stupid decision, see if this scenario sounds familiar to you.

I'm browsing the shoe department of a large department store when I spot the perfect pair of shoes. They're that rare combination of trendy (but not too trendy) and excellent quality (but not too expensive). I can already picture myself wearing them to work as well as a casual cocktail party—a true unicorn shoe, if you will.

I immediately find a shop assistant and ask for my size. As soon as he returns from the stockroom with that familiar frown on his face, my heart sinks. "Unfortunately, we're out of your size, but I brought you one size smaller just in case," he says. I consider my options, and eventually decide that I owe it to myself to *at least* try them on.

There's no doubt they're a little (okay, a lot) too tight, but they look a-ma-zing. So I buy them. Irresponsible? Maybe. But by the time I get home, I've convinced myself that I'll wear them *all the time* and that they'll probably stretch after a while anyway. Wishful thinking at its finest.

Unsurprisingly, they don't stretch. Despite this tiny inconvenient truth, however, I decide to take them for a spin the next night. I tell myself that after a glass (or two) of wine, I'll barely notice the fact that I can't feel my toes. An hour into the evening, I find myself awkwardly shifting from side to side, trying to mitigate the discomfort. Another hour later, I can feel the blisters starting to surface.

Why am I painting this seemingly irrelevant and increasingly gory picture for you?

Because this is what it's like to live out of alignment with your purpose. Initially, it's only slightly uncomfortable. You keep willing the job, relationship, environment, or—in my case—the shoe to fit. But no matter how strong your willpower is, or how badly you want it to work out, the discomfort continues to grow—until eventually, the pain is so overwhelming that you want to jump out of your own skin. You get to the point where you have no option *but* to listen to what your body is trying to tell you. Yes, you know better. But knowing better doesn't always guarantee that you will *do* better.

Unfortunately, the passage from uncomfortable to unbearable can take anywhere from days or weeks (if you're lucky) to years or even decades. Most of us—myself included—have been programmed to "suck it up" and "stay the course," especially if the course involves something or someone that looks great on paper—a "shiny penny," if you will. Why would you do anything to mess up your ostensibly perfect career, fairytale romance, or enviable cocktail look, right? Wrong. It may sound like a worthwhile trade-off in the short term, but you will pay the price eventually.

You will wake up one day and wonder how the holy hell you got yourself into this mess. When did you start trying to squeeze yourself into a poor-fitting shoe—and why? When did you start living someone else's dream instead of your own? Come to think of it, do you even know what your own dreams are anymore?

I didn't. When my so-called "quarter-life crisis" hit, I was twenty-three and working at a global consulting firm in New York City. I was traveling three or four days a week, working sixteen-hour days, and having regular meltdowns in the office bathroom. It wasn't *all* bad, of course, and I will forever cherish the many lessons I learned and the lifelong friendships I built during this chapter of my life. Nonetheless, it's fair to say I wasn't exactly thriving. (If I'm being honest, I didn't even know that was an option.) Fortunately, I was presented with a get out of jail free card—more on this story later—and to this day, I am still surprised I had the chutzpah to escape. But I often wonder what would have happened if I didn't. And it isn't pretty. It may *look* pretty on the outside, but I know just how miserable I would have been behind the impressive facade.

Like any transition, my jump from the corporate world into the great unknown of entrepreneurship was messy. It was also isolating. Very few people understood why I had left a promising career after just two years to start a consulting firm from scratch with one of my best friends. It didn't help that our mission was to help iconic, legacy brands better understand "millennials"—a term that at the time still warranted an explanation. Instead of nods of approval and admiration, people would raise a quizzical eyebrow when I answered the inevitable "what do you do" question. I'm a little ashamed to admit that I would occasionally find myself dropping my past employer's name in conversation, just to get the street cred I felt I deserved.

Now, seven years later, I consider myself one of the lucky ones. I look around at my peers today and can't help but wonder whether they're feeling just as stuck or lost as I was. Let's get one thing straight, however: I am by no means pretending to have it all figured out. There are still plenty of days I question everything about everything. But what I have now that I lacked then is a compass. I know what it feels like to be operating as my best, brightest, most fulfilled self. I know what it feels like to live *on purpose*. This doesn't mean I manage to successfully do so all the time—or even 50 percent of the time, frankly—but as long as I have a point of reference, I can find my way back there.

I opened this chapter with a quote from the work of a man named Howard Thurman. Once described as "the overlooked civil rights hero" by CNN, Thurman had an enormous influence on some of the greatest changemakers of our time, including Martin Luther King Jr. He describes the internal compass I just referred to as "the genuine." In his 1980 commencement speech for the graduating class of Spellman College, Thurman said, "If you cannot hear the sound of the genuine in you, you will all of your life spend your days on the ends of strings that somebody else pulls."[1] In other words, if you're unable to connect to your inner compass, you will find yourself without clear direction and will therefore be far more susceptible to other people's opinions and desires.

On paper, I am about as qualified to write a book as I was to start a business in my early twenties. I've thought about letting my imposter syndrome win on numerous occasions. But then I think back to who I would have been if I hadn't taken that leap of faith seven years ago—if I hadn't listened to the "sound of the genuine" inside of me—and it compels me to keep going. Because even if I can help *one* more person discover what makes them "come alive" so they can free themselves from the strings that somebody else pulls and show up for the life they were meant to live, I believe the world will be a little better than I found it.

# INTRODUCTION

> "Today you are You, that is truer than true.
> There is no one alive who is Youer than You!
> —Dr. Seuss

Purpose: it's such a simple and straightforward word. If you asked a random stranger on the street to define what purpose means, they would probably do a decent job. It's not exactly SAT-worthy material, after all.

The *Oxford English Dictionary* defines purpose as "the reason for which something is done or created or for which something exists." That makes sense. It's easy to come up with the purpose of many of the objects or constructs we interact with on a daily basis. The purpose of a car is to transport people or objects from point A to point B. The purpose of a shoe is to protect your feet (or to make a fashion statement at a cocktail party, but we'll assume that's secondary). The purpose of a phone is to allow two people to communicate remotely. You get the picture.

However, if you were to ask that same random stranger, "What is the purpose of a human life?" you would most likely receive a blank stare or dismissive laugh in response. When faced with the question of what *you* or *I* are created to do—why we exist—the answer isn't as straightforward. The word "purpose" suddenly feels both impossibly elusive and unbearably loaded. But what if it doesn't have to be? What if the purpose of life is simply to learn to listen to the little voice that resides inside your head, your heart, or your gut? What if living on purpose were as effortless as figuring out what makes you feel and operate at your very best, then designing your life around those things?

It sounds too obvious and too good to be true . . . but what if it's not?

## ONE FULL SERVING OF LIFE, PLEASE

Before I share my definition of purpose and how to identify yours, let's take a step back. Why do billions of people continue to overlook or actively avoid the clues to finding their purpose? Why are they willing to live with the uncomfortable reality of blisters in an effort to squeeze themselves into a pair of unicorn shoes that don't fit?

For most people, the answer is unsatisfyingly simple: they've never paused to consider it. I didn't. I was going through life on autopilot, happily climbing my way up an invisible ladder. It never even crossed my mind to consider whether I was on the *right* ladder, or whether I even needed to be on a ladder to begin with. I could have easily continued along that path and been perfectly content without a purpose—until I knew better. Looking back, the saddest thing of all was that I had grown so accustomed to my ladder that I thought it was all there was, at least for me. I had no idea there were not only other ladders out there, but an entire universe of possible paths to explore. There were mountains to climb, lazy rivers to float down, and mazes to get lost in—life, as it turns out, is the ultimate "choose your own adventure" experience.

I imagine that my aha moment was akin to when mathematician and astronomer Nicolaus Copernicus proposed that the earth was not, in fact, the center of the universe. It's hard to wrap your head around such a massive assault on what you believe to be true. It takes time for us humans to acquaint ourselves with a new normal—which is why every year, thousands of people still attend the Flat Earth Conference to hear from global speakers who disagree with Copernicus's findings and still believe the world is a flat disc. It isn't easy to process a monumental shift in your reality. Consequently, most of us settle for less than we deserve simply because we cannot (or will not) see beyond our current frame of reference. We settle for a "compatible" partner or a "decent" job. We settle for "fine" because we have no idea that "fan-frickin-fabulous" is even an option. But you, dear reader, are different. You bought this book. You would rather be enlightened than ignorant, even if it's the more challenging path to take. Because why not? Why should you settle for anything less than a full serving of life? Preferably with a cherry on top.

## IF YOU KNOW, YOU KNOW

I'm going to do something a little unorthodox. I'm going to give you the SparkNotes version of the book right here in the introduction: the most surefire way to live life to the fullest—to access "fan-frickin-fabulous"—is to articulate your purpose. Your why. Because when you live *on purpose*—when you live with intention—everything you do is infused with a greater sense of meaning. There's a rhyme and reason to it all. The decisions you make, the jobs you do, the relationships you invest in *matter*. What is more satisfying than the assurance that what we do and how we live our lives *matters*?

So now you know the secret to making the most of what poet Mary Oliver called "your one wild and precious life." I encourage you to keep reading, however, because like most worthwhile pursuits, articulating and living in alignment with your purpose is easier said than done. Not because any of the individual steps are particularly arduous. (In fact, after reading this book, you'll probably wonder why so many people are still walking around *without* a sense of purpose, disconnected from their true potential.) But because purpose is, by nature, a squishy concept that is hard to pin down. I know this because I have built a career on helping Fortune 500 companies and individuals do exactly that: pin down their purpose.

I credit most of my professional success to three things: curiosity, impatience, and a tirelessly analytical mind. As a child, I would beg my parents to let me stay up past my bedtime so I could listen to the "adult conversations" that would take place in our living room. I was particularly fascinated by discussions about big, global challenges or complex interpersonal issues and wouldn't hesitate to chime in with my diagnosis or recommended course of action. What originally drew me to a career in consulting was the promise of solving problems for a living. While it may have temporarily squashed my creativity, the training I received sharpened my analytical muscle and gave me the confidence to break down any problem in a systematic way. It's one of my superpowers. Tell me your desired outcome, and I will prescribe the most efficient path to get there. This is what ultimately led me to develop a formula for purpose: a repeatable, structured process that allows companies to identify and articulate their unique reason for being.

It wasn't until I started my own personal development journey, however, that I considered how this same formula might apply to individuals. As I consumed every self-help book and podcast I could get my hands on, I soon discovered that there were very few methods that spoke to people like me—people who need a methodical, step-by-step approach to something as ethereal as purpose. Selling all your belongings and traveling the world to "find yourself" or investing your life savings in a self-help guru's seminar isn't exactly a realistic proposition for most. While I wholeheartedly believe that these things can help *some* people find their purpose, it's not exactly a universal solution. It took some tweaking, but eventually I was able to adapt the model we used with our clients to help individuals articulate their purpose too. That's how the Find Your Purpose workshop was born. Over the past three years, my colleagues and I have facilitated the workshop for entrepreneurs, corporate employees, parents, students, and freelancers all across the world—both in person and online.

This book is a summary of everything I've learned along the way: it's a practical roadmap to purpose that *anyone* can follow, whether this is your first foray into personal development or you have a crystal collection at home and a psychic on speed dial. No matter where you are in your journey, this book will offer both guidance and accountability. You will need both in spades because the path to purpose requires a willingness to admit to your own bullshit, to break down the walls you've so carefully built up around you, and to stop "shoulding" all over yourself: "I *should* take this job."

"I *should* spend more time with this person." "I *should* be excited about this opportunity." This type of brutal honesty does not come naturally to most of us, but it's essential if you want to see results.

Another unfortunate reality of purpose is that it cannot be achieved by sheer force. You cannot hustle your way to purpose. (Believe me, I've tried.) Instead of effort, this journey requires an unwavering faith. Faith that you are indeed the master of your own destiny. Faith that you are not a victim of your life, but a steward of it. Faith that you are not defined by your circumstances, but by how you respond to them. Upholding this type of faith is challenging, especially when life inevitably throws a few shitstorms your way. I guarantee you that while weathering these storms, it will seem a lot easier to ditch your dreams, accept the cards you've been dealt, and tell yourself to "grow up" or "get real." You will be tempted to settle for *surviving* life rather than *thriving* in it.

The process I will lay out in the coming chapters is designed to help you prepare for and navigate the unpredictable, often tumultuous journey to purpose. There will be roadblocks, detours, and many enticing offramps trying to lure you from the highlighted route. You will be challenged to recalibrate and reorient yourself in the right direction, over and over again. Every time you do, your internal compass—what Howard Thurman called "the sound of the genuine in you"—will get a little bit stronger and a little less sensitive to external distractions.

## THE LAY OF THE LAND

This book is organized into three parts. Part One will lay the groundwork for what's to come. We will explore what purpose is and what it is not, and how discovering your purpose has the potential to transform your life. Part Two is where I put you to work. I will guide you through a series of "Discovery Missions" to help you peel back the layers of conditioning you've unconsciously adopted over the years. You will learn to trust your inner voice, increase your self-awareness, and recognize the clues that are pointing you towards your own North Star. By the end of Part Two, you will be able to clearly articulate what it takes for you to come alive.

Part Three is where the rubber meets the road. This is where you start to marry intention with action in order to redesign your life around what matters most. It is also what sets this formula apart from other methodologies. I included this final section after noticing how challenging this part of the journey is for even the most well-intentioned purpose seekers. They can wrap their head around the importance of purpose, and perhaps even define what it would look like for them to live a meaningful life, but taking action and holding themselves accountable is a whole different kettle of fish. To set you up for success, I will cover some of the most common roadblocks and offer tactical tips on how to overcome them. I will also introduce you to some of the practices and rituals I found most helpful on my own journey. Next, I will offer advice on how to infuse more purpose into four of the most important dimensions of your life: Work, Relationships, Play, and Money. Finally, I will share one of my favorite tools: The Purpose Plan. This framework will help you break down big goals into concrete action steps so you can create your very own roadmap to purpose.

There is no "right" way to approach this book. While I

recommend that you complete the exercises in Part Two in one session if possible, the rest is meant to be evergreen. My hope is that you continue to revisit this material often, as your circumstances and your purpose will evolve over time.

While finding your purpose is designed to be a solo adventure, it can be incredibly powerful to go through this process alongside a group or an accountability buddy. Most of the work will be deeply personal, but it can be helpful to have a safe space in which to troubleshoot roadblocks or brainstorm new paths. When facilitating this material in a retreat setting, I am always struck by the accelerated growth that takes place when people find themselves in a supportive community of likeminded individuals who are all searching for greater fulfillment together.

## WIIFM

I used to think of myself as a horrible sales person. The process of convincing someone to buy something or donate to a certain cause made me feel terribly uncomfortable. I didn't see how I could accomplish my goal without coming across as pushy or sleazy. That is, until I learned about the marketing acronym WIIFM: What's in it for me? The best marketers and sales people are able to put themselves in their customers' shoes and clearly articulate how a particular product, service, or donation will transform their lives for the better. Every marketing asset or communication is focused on answering that question. WIIFM completely shifted my perspective on sales: instead of viewing my pitches as acts of persuasion, I started viewing them as acts of service. I have the opportunity to introduce someone to something that can change their lives, and it is *my job* to paint a picture of that potential future in the most captivating, truthful way. If I can do that, I have done my job well—the decision of whether the pretty picture is worth the price tag is still up to them, after all. In the case of this book, I have witnessed the transformative power of this process many, many times over—in myself, as well as in others. As such, my *what's in it for you* pitch is inspired by *real* stories about *real* people who have reoriented their lives around what matters most.

The caveat to this journey is that there is no final destination. For those of us who choose to live on purpose—who choose to thrive instead of survive—the road never ends. But waiting for you *along* this path is a life beyond your wildest dreams. A life that makes you giddy with excitement every morning for what the day might bring. A life that is so fulfilling that when you scroll through your social feed, you can actually feel joy for other people instead of resentment or jealousy. A life that makes you feel like you are exactly where you're meant to be, doing exactly what you're meant to do. A life that enables you to draw on your many talents and overcome your deepest fears. A life that inspires you to show up as your best, most authentic self for the ones you love. A life worth living.

Want to know the best part? By living fearlessly and ferociously in alignment with your own purpose, you will inspire others to do the same. People around you will want a piece of whatever you're snacking on. They will recognize their own potential, simply by seeing how you're living up to yours. By doing this work, you can not only change your *own* reality, but someone else's too.

So fasten your seatbelt and get ready for the ride of a lifetime.

# CHAPTER ONE

# WHAT A TIME TO BE ALIVE

For as long as humans have walked this earth, we've been asking ourselves the question: Why are we here? What's the point of this whole circus? The quest for purpose is nothing new. Many of the most brilliant minds in history dedicated their lives to solving this puzzle, dating all the way back to classical antiquity. Naturally, there have been eras when survival took precedence over pondering purpose—times during which war, exploration, trade, and industrialization consumed every last ounce of people's mental and physical capacity. Purpose could wait.

Today, however, we find ourselves in a period of prolonged prosperity. While some of the distractions still exist, brilliant innovations in technology and healthcare mean that we are no longer solely focused on survival. Over the past two hundred years, life expectancy in the developed world has doubled (per the UN Population Division). A longer life expectancy inspired a whole new stage of life we now refer to as "retirement." (I recognize this concept is only a reality in the most privileged of societies, but if you're reading this book, I'm willing to bet you know what I'm talking about.) According to this privileged new normal, the first third of your life is generally dedicated to education, the second third to work, and the final third to freedom. Freedom to choose where you live and how you spend your time and money. Freedom to ask yourself what matters most to you and design a life that is oriented around that thing—be it grandchildren, fishing, or travel. Retirement has given our parents and grandparents the freedom to explore these big, probing questions again, in the absence of distractions. But I can't help but wonder: Why wait until the last third of our lives to start living this way? What makes someone "deserve" that type of freedom at the arbitrary age of sixty-five?

At the risk of sounding like a stereotypical millennial, I don't believe there's anything *wrong* with having our cake and eating it too. Especially if you're willing to put your head down and hustle stupidly hard for that piece of cake. In fact, I'm very proud to be part of a generation that is constantly pushing boundaries and questioning the status quo. We refuse to work from nine to five, stay at the same job for twenty years, or prioritize profit over purpose simply because someone somewhere says so. We refuse to believe we can't do well *and* do good simultaneously. Of course, the only reason we can afford to have this mindset is because our parents and grandparents paved the way. Without the tremendous economic progress they achieved, we wouldn't have the tools or the means to pioneer a new way of life. They also (perhaps unintentionally) granted us permission to do things differently. They were the ones who encouraged us to dream big and become whomever we wanted to be. (Fortunately for us, they forgot to add the caveat "as long as that includes a stable career, predictable hours, and a mortgage.")

The truth is that our generation is no more eager to live on purpose than our parents and grandparents were at our age. We *are,* however, less patient (thank you, social media!) and, yes, perhaps a little more entitled. But consider for a moment that this perceived weakness may be one of our greatest strengths. This restlessness, paired with equal amounts of intolerance and idealism, may be exactly what's required for humanity to take its next big leap forward.

## ASK THE BIG QUESTIONS

One of my favorite questions to ask someone my senior is what advice they would give their younger self. The responses vary, but over the years I've detected a pattern. Those under fifty years old will often share practical advice: "Seek out mentors in your field." "Start investing in the stock market sooner." "Choose a partner based on shared values, not shared interests." These are all important insights, don't get me wrong. The advice from those over fifty, however, is a tad less tactical and more hedonistic in nature: "Stop wasting your time on frivolous goals or achievements that don't matter." "Focus on the people you care about most." "Don't worry so much about what other people think." Without fail, their advice comes down to one key principle: *enjoy life*. In other words, do things that *feel good*. The operative word being *feel* rather than *look* or *sound* good.

Bronnie Ware is an Australian author and motivational speaker who started her career as a palliative caregiver. She became famous for a blog post she published in 2009 called "Regrets of the Dying." In the post, she describes the top five regrets her patients shared on their deathbeds. The two most prevalent regrets were, "I wish I'd had the courage to live a life true to myself, not the life others expected of me," and, "I wish I hadn't worked so hard."[2] Think about that for a moment. As you get closer to meeting your maker, you realize how short and precious your time here on earth really is. Suddenly, the years you spent at a job that felt "meh" or with a partner whom you knew wasn't "the one" seem like a colossal waste of time. Of course, those experiences shaped you into the person you are today—yet, if you knew what you know now, could you have accelerated the learning process just a little?

There is absolutely *no reason* we should have to wait until retirement to ask ourselves what truly lights us up inside. What if you could discover your purpose in the *first* third of your life, so you can make the rest of it *that much more* meaningful? What if you could study something that fascinates you, instead of something that looks good on a resume? What if you could earn a living doing something you love and something that is a hundred percent aligned with your values, instead of something that simply pays the bills or puts your degree to good use? What if you exclusively had relationships that fill you up rather than deplete you? What if you only spent your money on the things that bring you joy? What if you no longer had to ask yourself "what if"?

## NO MORE WHAT IFS

I love lists. But what I love even more than making lists is checking items off them. The sense of satisfaction I feel after completing a task is pathetic, but nonetheless extremely motivating to me. You can imagine how this obsession has impacted my life.

I grew up in a small town in the Netherlands outside of

Amsterdam. Even as a young girl, I had a fire in my belly to do something *big*, something that *mattered*. Instead of asking myself what mattered *to me*, however, I looked toward the people that pop culture, my parents, and society had dubbed "successful." At age eleven, I created a list of life goals that I thought would guarantee my success. Then I started to work my way down the list. Graduate from high school cum laude, check. Attend an Ivy League school, check. Become the captain of a Division I sports team, check. Get a job at a top management consulting firm, check. I am not sharing this list of achievements to boast—I am very aware of the role good fortune and circumstance played in my story. The point is that not once did I question whether these goals aligned with the life I wanted to lead or the talents I had been blessed with.

Fast-forward a decade, and my twenty-three-year-old self is working sixteen-hour days on the nineteenth floor of an office building in the middle of Times Square. (Ironically, I had always dreamed of moving to New York City when I was younger. Except in that version of my dream, I was an actress on Broadway, not a management consultant.) There was absolutely nothing "wrong" with my life. I was working with brilliant people and solving big, important problems. Sure, I wasn't exactly excited to go to work every day and would spend my weekends glued to my BlackBerry, but I thought that was simply the price you pay for "success." Besides, I was working so much that I barely had any time to consider what the alternative might be.

I was just starting to think about checking my next box—an MBA—when a close college friend of mine moved back to the city. She told me about an idea she had for a business, and I was instantly intrigued. Soon, we were meeting before and after work. I would sneak out of the office to join her for meetings across town, and I distinctly remember sprinting down Seventh Avenue one blisteringly hot day in August to make it back to work for a partner meeting. My friend and I had just finished our first big pitch, and I was exhilarated. I must have looked like a crazy woman. Dripping sweat, bag flailing, stopping every few seconds to shove a heel back into my skimpy flats. That was the first moment I let myself consider what life would be like if I jumped off the proverbial cliff. A few months later, my friend asked me to join her full time as a cofounder. I jumped head first. If you would have asked me (or anyone who knew me, for that matter) if I would leave my job at a reputable firm for a startup that had no funding, no clients, no health insurance, and no team or track record to speak of, the answer would have most certainly been no. I had never been much of a thrill-seeker, but the fire in my belly had been stoked. Our brainstorming sessions and early pitch meetings opened my eyes to a new reality—a reality that made me come alive in a way my "perfect" job did not.

For the first time in a long time, this feeling trumped any desire I had to check a box. I knew it was a risk, but it didn't faze me, nor did the fear of what others might think. I had gotten a taste of what it would be like to be my own boss, to see the impact I was having on others, and to spend my time on things that truly mattered to me. I had gotten my first glimpse of what it would be like to live *on purpose*.

# CHAPTER TWO

# *WHAT PURPOSE IS AND WHAT IT IS NOT*

> " *He who knows the why for his existence*
> *will be able to bear almost any how.* "
> —Viktor Frankl

If you're still a little fuzzy on how to define purpose (particularly *your* purpose), it might help to unpack what purpose is *not*.

## PURPOSE IS NOT A SINGLE VOCATION OR OCCUPATION

The word purpose is inextricably tied to intention. When you act *with a* purpose or *on* purpose, you do something with a specific intent in mind. In other words, you have a clear sense of *why* you are doing something. In his bestselling book *Start with Why*, Simon Sinek introduces his readers to the concept of the Golden Circle. He shares that most companies and leaders start with the outermost circle: *what* they do. Next, they move on to *how* they do it, and finally *why* they do what they do. Sinek suggests, however, that the world's most inspiring companies and leaders move in the exact opposite direction. They start by getting crystal clear on their *why* before moving on to *how* and *what*. Sinek often refers to technology giant Apple to illustrate this counterintuitive approach. Instead of leading with *what*—in their case, computers—Apple has always focused on *why*: an unflappable desire to challenge the status quo. This raison d'être is reflected in their brand, their product, and their people. (Few leaders are as notorious for going against the grain as the late Apple founder Steve Jobs.) *How* they challenge the status quo is by offering customers a clean, crisp experience that is unlike any other technology company.

Think about it. If Dell or HP were to copy Apple's less-is-more packaging design or elegant user interface, would these companies resonate with consumers in the same way? Most likely not. Not because the product is any different, but because the intention—the *why*—behind this design does not feel authentic. Dell and HP have never been challengers.

This applies to your purpose as well. *How* you pursue your purpose and *what* activities or jobs you do in pursuit of that purpose can (and likely will) change over time. You can switch positions, companies, or industries, all while living in accordance with the same purpose. It's not *what* you do, it's *why* you do it that matters. You can live in alignment with your purpose as a painter, an Uber driver, or an investment banker. Your sense of purpose need not (and should not) be derived from your job title. In fact, it doesn't need to be derived from your job at all. There are plenty of other ways to live on purpose. If Apple were to pivot to making water bottles, their customers would simply start buying water bottles from them instead of computers. Consumers would inherently trust that these water bottles would be unlike any other water bottle on the market. Why? Because otherwise Apple wouldn't bother. The company has never wavered from their commitment to doing things differently. We tend to place far too much significance on the *what* and the *how*, when the only thing worth worrying about— the only thing that truly endures—is *why*.

Let's take my friend Sara, for example. For as long as she can remember, all Sara has wanted to do is serve others. As a young girl, she would join her mother when she volunteered at the local hospital, delivering flowers and well-wishes to the patients. She would watch the nurses in awe as they administered medicine, comforted family members, and checked off their charts. No one was surprised when Sara announced she wanted to attend nursing school at age eighteen. This became her *what*. Fast-forward a decade, and Sara wakes up one day to the uncomfortable realization that she no longer enjoys being a nurse. She can't quite articulate why, but it doesn't give her the same sense of fulfillment it once did. She continues to go to work with a heavy heart. She feels stuck. Leaving her job would mean letting everyone down—her parents (who invested in her education), her patients, her colleagues—not to mention herself. Sara had always been the steadfast one, the friend and daughter no one had to worry about. She asked herself, Why start causing drama now? Besides, who would she be without her scrubs? Sara's identity was so tied up in her profession that she truly believed that being a nurse was the *only* way to live in alignment with her purpose, the *only* way to serve people. Athletes who suffer from career-ending injuries experience the same reckoning: Who am I if I'm not out there competing?

The answer lies in the old adage "many roads lead to Rome." Being a nurse is just *one* of many ways Sara can live out her purpose. She can become a teacher, a physical therapist, a caregiver, a masseuse—or, as she discovered, a social worker. By mistaking your purpose for a specific vocation, you are unnecessarily torturing yourself. By rigidly clinging to the *what,* you may miss out on an opportunity to live out your purpose in a way that is even more joyful for you. Sara certainly didn't miss her grueling schedule and aching body. As you embark on this journey, I encourage you to keep an open mind and let go of the *whats* and *hows* you consciously or unconsciously have come to identify with. Instead, focus on pinpointing your *why:* what is it about a particular job that sets your soul on fire? Because at the end of the day, the only constant in life is change. Your job will change, your environment will change, the people you surround yourself with will change. But as long as you remain committed to your purpose, you will thrive no matter the circumstance.

## PURPOSE IS NOT A DESTINATION

I hate to break it to you, but you might be in for a long ride. If you're lucky, that is. The path to purpose is never-ending. It's a lifelong journey. You don't "achieve" your purpose one day, only to go back to living a purposeless life the next. I like to think of the path to purpose as your highlighted route on a GPS system. Once you enter "purpose" as the destination, you will spend the rest of your life reorienting yourself toward this true north. (Don't worry, this will feel a lot less daunting after reading this book.) There are plenty of other routes to take through life—and you will surely find yourself on these at times—but the highlighted route is the *best one*. Not because it is the most direct or smoothest route, but because it happens to be the most rewarding. It holds the greatest potential for growth and fulfillment.

You might be wondering, if there's no destination, then what's the rush? What's the point in accelerating your journey to purpose? Why *not* wait until you're sixty-five? Because life doesn't come with guarantees. The only guarantee we have is the present moment, and the sooner you can articulate your purpose, the sooner you can make each and every moment count. Unfortunately, most of us prefer to live in denial about this truth. We spend most of our time fixated on the past or the future. That is, until a life-threatening illness, near-death experience, or loss of a loved one reminds us how fragile life can be and how we can't afford to take it for granted.

My mother died of breast cancer when I was ten years old. She had successfully fought it off in her early thirties, but the cancer returned with a vengeance at age thirty-six, and we said our goodbyes just a few months after her thirty-eighth birthday. I was heartbroken, but I never felt like a victim. Not because I was a particularly enlightened ten-year-old, but because I instinctively knew that my mom lived every last moment *on purpose*. Her illness enabled her to identify and embrace her "why" with open arms and without hesitation. This gave her a magnetic quality. No matter what room she stepped into, people would gravitate towards her. To this day, twenty years later, strangers still come up to my siblings and me to share stories about how she impacted their lives. She made quite an impression in her short time on earth.

A few months before my mom passed away, she lived out one of her greatest dreams: to record a CD. She had always loved to sing and often performed at family weddings or events, but there was something about being in a real recording studio that excited her beyond belief. When she got sick again, her personal mantra became "live life to the fullest." She followed her own advice and recorded a CD titled *The Sound of Life*. In between each track, she shares a short reflection on her song choices. Before the very last song, she says: "If you harbor any dream, don't just dream it, go ahead and do it." That is her legacy. That was her purpose. She was here to inspire those around her to stop playing small. She is also the reason I started writing this book.

People often say life's too short, but it doesn't have to be. How you spend your time—whether you live to be thirty-eight or eighty-three—is entirely up to you. If you choose to live on purpose, you can find fulfillment in the smallest, most mundane moments. You can learn to let go of the end goal—the destination—and discover the magic that can be found along the way. Life is not a race or a battle—it's a privilege. So it's up to you: you can take an easier, less rewarding route; you can postpone your purpose journey until it's more convenient, thereby accepting the risk that you may never have the opportunity to start; or you can take the wheel and follow the instructions to your highlighted route.

## PURPOSE DOES NOT EQUAL HAPPINESS

The two are often used interchangeably, but it's important to understand the nuances. Happiness is a temporary state of being, while purpose is an enduring motive: it's unwavering, like the North Star. (Because of its location vis-à-vis earth, the North Star—or Polaris— appears to be the only star that maintains a fixed position. As a result, it's often used as a compass for navigational purposes.) Studies have found that people tend to measure a "happy life" by a lack of stress or worry. If that's the case, it is possible that purpose can be pursued *at the expense* of someone's happiness. Sometimes you have to sacrifice short-term happiness for long-term fulfill- ment. New moms, for example, often say they have a greater sense of purpose than ever before, even if their wellbeing has taken a hit due to repeated sleepless nights and a complete loss of control over their bodies and schedules. Similarly, someone starting a new business might be under a tremendous amount of stress to raise funds, hire the right team, and source the right vendors—yet they have never felt more alive. Notice that in both examples the indi- vidual is acting in the service of something other or greater than themselves. Purpose implies contribution—feeling useful, valued, worthy—while happiness does not.

So, if purpose does not equal happiness, what does it equal? How can we measure the outcome of living on purpose? The an- swer is by looking at life satisfaction. There is evidence suggesting that people with a clear sense of purpose rate their overall life sat- isfaction significantly higher than those who lack purpose.[3] The difference between happiness and life satisfaction, in my experi- ence, is context. When you ask someone if they're happy, they typ- ically respond based on how stress-free or worry-free their life is *at that specific moment in time.* When you ask someone to self-report on their life satisfaction, however, they will usually take the bigger picture into account. They might consider situational factors such as their age, the global economic climate, the obstacles they've had to overcome, and the lessons they've learned as a result. In other words, they're asking themselves: *Given the circumstances, am I satisfied with where I'm at?*

As you can imagine, a life satisfaction score is more likely to endure over time compared to the happiness metric. For example, if you asked me to rate my happiness levels around 8:00 a.m. on any given morning (assuming I had a good night's sleep), I would probably answer with a nine out of ten. But let's say that I get into my car half an hour later and realize the battery is dead. I have to take an Uber to work and am running late for an important meeting. My happiness rating drops to a seven out of ten. At work, I receive an email from one of my top prospective clients regretfully telling me that they've decided to go in a different direction. I spend the rest of the day lamenting the time I wasted on the proposal, trying to figure out how to convince the prospect otherwise and imagining all the possible doomsday scenarios that might occur if I can't. By the time I get home that night, my happiness rating has dropped to a four out of ten.

If you had asked me to rate my life satisfaction on that same day, however, my score might only drop a single point between morning to night. I would rationalize that while I might have lost my top prospect, I am still incredibly fortunate to work for myself, to have a roof over my head, a husband I love, and a life I used to dream of. I would look beyond the emotions I was experiencing in the moment and contextualize the situation.

I started this chapter with a quote from Viktor Frankl's profound book *Man's Search for Meaning*. He wrote the book after spending almost three years in German concentration camps during World War II. As a prisoner, he observed that what consistently separated those who survived the Holocaust from those who perished was their ability to recognize a higher purpose. Frankl was in no way diminishing the suffering he and others experienced, but he was able to ascribe meaning to it, and this allowed him to persevere.

It's easy to get caught up in the pursuit of happiness, following the trail of dopamine hits that accompany those moments of bliss. But happiness is fickle. It can be fleeting and is often influenced by things beyond your control like the weather, someone else's mood, or an empty car battery. After the war, Frankl went on to create logotherapy, a form of psychotherapy that is based on the assumption that while people cannot control their circumstances, they *can* control how they choose to respond to these circumstances. Do you concede, or do you rise to the occasion? Do you give up, or do you choose to make lemonade out of lemons? Life satisfaction is determined entirely by your attitude. As Frankl discovered, having a strong conviction in your why—your purpose—makes it infinitely easier to approach any situation, no matter how dire, as an opportunity for growth.

## SO WHAT IS PURPOSE?

We covered the official dictionary definition of purpose in the introduction: "the reason for which something is done or created or for which something exists." But this definition is far more suitable for describing the purpose of *things* rather than *people*. Instead, I like to define purpose like this:

> Your purpose is the sweet spot where your passions, your strengths, and your potential to contribute intersect.

Put simply, pursuing your purpose in life comes down to figuring out how to contribute to the world around you in a meaningful way by doing something that you love, and something that you happen to be *pretty* good at. That's your sweet spot. (I say "pretty" good, because if you're anything like me, you're your own worst critic and will most likely be the last person on earth to recognize something as a personal "strength." This method will require you to, however.)

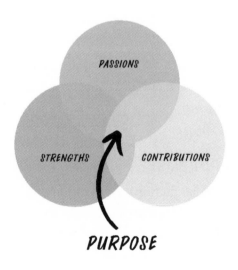

Let's unpack this definition. First of all, your **passions** are the things in life you can't help but be drawn to. They're the stuff that makes you lose track of time. They're the stuff that someone can wake you up for in the middle of the night. They're the stuff you can't shut up about. They're the stuff you spend too much money on (but they're always worth it). They're the stuff you are endlessly curious about.

Your **strengths** are your superpowers—the God-given talents that come naturally to you, as well as the hard-earned skills you've honed over time. Because we don't always recognize (or admit to) our own strengths, the best place to look is outside yourself. What do other people ask for your advice on? What do they rely on you for? What have people complimented you on? In addition to the hard skills (for example, your culinary prowess, your legal expertise, or your organizational skills), consider the softer skills (your ability to listen, your ability to make someone feel instantly at ease, or your strong sense of intuition). We tend to undervalue these softer strengths in ourselves, even though they are the first things we acknowledge in someone else.

The final (often overlooked) piece of the puzzle is **contributions**. This refers to the impact you have on the world and the people around you. Contributions are essential to purpose, because humans are designed to thrive when we're acting in service of something greater than ourselves. We crave feeling useful. We crave feeling needed. While a lot of purpose-oriented articles or frameworks touch on passions and strengths in a variety of ways, very few consider this critical aspect. In my humble opinion, however, only when you apply your passions and your strengths to a cause that is meaningful to you do they translate to purpose. I am referring to "cause" here in the broadest possible sense of the word—it does not have to be a specific initiative or nonprofit. Let me illustrate my point.

## PURPOSE IN PRACTICE

This is not about finding the perfect recipe for purpose; it's about identifying the right ingredients *for you*. Once you're able to define these inputs—your passions, strengths, and potential to contribute—you can start to experiment with the many possible combinations that might result in a magical, mouthwatering meal.

I first met Mac at the kitchen table of an old farmhouse in Princeton, New Jersey. Mac had purchased the farm back in 1962, and today—almost six decades later—it's home to his son, daughter-in-law, and their four girls. Mac and his wife had recently moved back into the house when it became clear that they required a little extra care. By the time I met Mac, he was approaching ninety. I remember exactly what he wore as he jumped out of his seat to greet me: he was sporting a cotton button-down, worn jeans, cowboy boots, and a Marine Corps belt. Despite his frail frame and the deep grooves in his skin, Mac's cheeky grin radiated a youthful curiosity while his smiling eyes suggested a gentlemanly charm that was instantly disarming. I, like many others who had the pleasure of meeting Mac, was smitten.

On the surface, Mac lived a simple life. He would start every day by collecting the paper at the end of the driveway and spend the morning reading it from front to back, occasionally cutting out an article he thought a family member might enjoy. When his wife had dolled herself up for the day, he would graciously escort her down to breakfast with the same sense of pride as a groom walking his new bride down the aisle. The rest of the day was dedicated to running errands, mowing the lawn, or visiting friends. Evenings were spent in front of the television watching a ball game with a bowl of ice cream. The next day, Mac would rinse and repeat. It was hardly Hollywood blockbuster material. Yet, the more time I spent with Mac, the more extraordinary he became.

Mac enlisted in the Marine Corps in 1942, shortly after graduating college. He served as a bomber pilot in the Pacific during World War II, where he was decorated with six Air Medals and two Distinguished Flying Crosses. Humble as he was, the stories of his bravery were always told by others while he blushed stoically. When the war ended, he moved to Texas and met the love of his life. Their marriage puts even the most epic romance novels to shame—seventy-three years later, she was still the center of his universe. After leaving the military, he embarked on a career in newspaper advertising, where Mac's entrepreneurial leadership and ability to form fast friendships served him well. In addition to baseball, he was deeply devoted to his faith, his family, and his community.

I may have met Mac during the epilogue of his life, but it was clear that he had mastered his list of ingredients. After a life of experimentation, he was still finding new recipes—new ways to operate in his sweet spot. Instead of playing ball or coaching Little League, he now enjoyed watching the professionals from the comfort of his couch; instead of selling newspaper ads, reading his favorite paper became the highlight of his day; instead of serving his country, he now served his community as an elder in the local church. Mac was uncompromising when it came to what he valued in life, and continued to find ways to contribute to the people and the causes dear to his heart. He may not have made headlines, but boy did he live *on purpose*. Every day of his life, Mac made time for his passions and drew on his many talents to make the lives of those in his vicinity just a little bit better. Mac's legacy is not measured in anything particularly remarkable, like the number of newspapers he sold or the number of home runs he hit—or even the number of medals he was awarded. Mac's legacy is measured in the number of community gatherings he hosted, the number of embraces he shared with his wife, the number of winks he exchanged with his grandchildren across the kitchen table, and his ability to make perfect strangers, like myself, feel like old friends.

In summary, your purpose = your sweet spot = your *why*. Throughout this book, I will use these words interchangeably. When you're living in your sweet spot—doing something you love, something you're good at, and something that makes an impact on the world around you—you're living *on purpose*. You are a reflection of your most authentic self. It's as "simple" as that. Your purpose is not a singular or fixed concept. There are many different ways you can operate in your sweet spot—just like there are many different recipes that result in a delicious meal, even if the ingredients remain the same. When you've discovered your sweet spot, you are inherently operating with a strong sense of *why*. You are motivated by something greater than the ego, something greater than yourself. Your purpose is the reason you keep showing up. It's not a job, a person, or any one achievement. It's your essence. Your fuel. It's the thread that connects everything you value in life. It's the wind beneath your wings. It's what makes you come alive.

## STRENGTHS FINDER EXERCISE

If you're struggling to identify your strengths, try this. Reach out to three people you trust and have spent considerable time with over the past twelve months. Ask them to answer the following two questions:

- What am I better at than anyone else you know?

- When is the last time you saw me shine? What was I doing?

Let them know you are conducting a self-evaluation and would appreciate their honest, timely feedback. It's imperative that you keep an open mind when it comes to the responses you receive, as you may be surprised at how other people perceive you.

## GET COMFORTABLE BEING UNCOMFORTABLE

If this whole "finding your purpose" thing feels daunting or overwhelming to you, that's because it is. If it were easy, everyone would be living out their purpose and there would be a lot less suffering, addiction, anxiety, and prescription drugs—to name just a few of the ways humans are trying to numb the discomfort they feel. It's not that it's complicated—it's actually a very simple process—but it requires us to do things most of us prefer to avoid, such as admitting to our deepest, darkest desires; facing our fears head on; and venturing beyond our comfort zone. In one of the most-watched TED Talks to date, author and researcher Brené Brown talks about the difference between those who live whole-heartedly—those who feel a sense of love and belonging—and those who don't. She discovered that what sets the whole-hearted apart is their willingness to be vulnerable. They are able to put themselves out there, with no assurance that the gamble will pay off. They are willing to let go of who they believe they *should* be in order to become who they really are. Living on purpose requires you to operate in your sweet spot, even when (especially when) it's the path of *most* resistance. Living on purpose requires you to become comfortable with feeling vulnerable.

But why put yourself through that? Why risk falling flat on your face?

Because striving for anything less than a fulfilling life is a waste of your time. Living on purpose doesn't guarantee rainbows and unicorns all day every day. It can be incredibly challenging, uncomfortable, and isolating. It can bring you to your knees and turn your world upside down. And yet, studies continue to show that people with a greater sense of purpose perform at a higher level than their counterparts. They experience better sleep[4], better health indicators[5], and even enjoy better relationships[6]. It's hard to pinpoint one specific reason, but here's my personal take. People who live on purpose—like Frankl, my mother, and Mac—live without leaving anything on the table. They live wholeheartedly. This brings an enormous sense of calm. If they were to die tomorrow, they would feel confident that they showed up and took full advantage of the gifts they were given. They would die knowing that they embraced vulnerability and overcame fear in the service of something greater. But it's not just about how we feel at the end of our lives. Living in alignment with your purpose allows you to experience more magic and more joy in the everyday. It allows you to do what feels good to you in the moment, without getting hung up on what might *look* or *sound* good to others. It allows you to stop torturing yourself. It allows you to stop sweating the small stuff.

Before we dive into finding, articulating, and living out your purpose, I want to address one final question that comes up quite often: what if I don't have a purpose? Perhaps you struggled to come up with any passions or strengths when you first read about the sweet spot framework. Or perhaps you have no idea what cause(s) you care about. Whatever your starting point is, know this: *everyone* has a purpose. Yes, even you—no matter how lost or uninspired you feel right now. Nature doesn't make mistakes. You were born to play your part in this binge-worthy reality show we call life. Your existence is not a coincidence, nor are the activities and the people you are drawn to. The real question is whether you can be courageous enough to follow the blueprint I will present in this book so you can become the person you were born to be. In the words of my favorite self-help queen, Oprah Winfrey: "Everybody has a calling, and your real job in life is to figure out as soon as possible what that is, who you were meant to be, and begin to honor that in the best way possible for yourself." Rest assured, this book will help you take the first important steps.

PART TWO

# FIND YOUR PURPOSE

# CHAPTER THREE

# REMEMBER HOW TO LISTEN

"*Your life is always speaking to you.*"
—Oprah Winfrey

Here's the good news: you already know what your purpose is. Let that sink in for a moment. So why the heck did I buy this book then? you might be wondering. Because, chances are, this knowledge is buried so deep inside your subconscious that you aren't even aware it's there. And even if you *are* aware of it, you probably have no idea where to start searching for this information—or what to do with the information once you find it. Don't worry, that's what Part Two of the playbook is all about. It's like a beginner's guide to the game of purpose, filled with tactics and plays to help you navigate this sometimes rocky, but always rewarding, road.

If you were born in the late 1980s or early 1990s, you likely once were (or still are) the proud owner of a Beanie Baby collection. My favorite thing about these creatures is the little tag that comes attached to their ear. The tag features the Beanie Baby's name, date of birth, and a short poem that describes—in essence—its purpose.

Let's take little Halo, for example:

Halo
DATE OF BIRTH: August 31, 1998
When you sleep, I'm always here
Don't be afraid, I am near
Watching over you with lots of love
Your guardian angel from up above

It's brilliant. There's absolutely no question as to what Halo's mission is here on earth. Can you imagine if human babies came with a tag like that too?

Trey
DATE OF BIRTH: January 5, 1990
I was blessed with an analytical mind
You may be surprised by the connections I'll find
I am happiest when solving a big, juicy mystery
And am destined for a life of incessant inquiry

No such luck, unfortunately. We humans have to find our purpose without any clues. Or do we? While it may not be as succinct as a four-line poem, we are all born with an incredibly powerful purpose detector that is constantly offering us helpful hints. The trouble is that most of us were never told that we possess this tool, let alone how to operate it.

The tool I'm referring to is your inner voice (also known as your intuition or your gut). The word "voice" can be misleading because it is rarely as loud and clear as someone speaking to you in the flesh. In fact, in some cases, your inner voice may communicate through other sensations such as feelings or smells, rather than words. Your inner voice is that deep knowing you experience or the words you hear (but no one else can) before your rational mind can create a story to make sense of it. It's the instantaneous, inexplicable response your body has to a person or situation it encounters. Have you ever met someone and instantly known you would become great friends? Have you ever avoided an accident because you felt an unexplained urge to take an alternate route home? Have you ever felt the sudden desire to reach out to someone only to discover that person was in desperate need of a friend? These are all examples of your inner voice at work.

It has taken me decades to get friendly with my inner voice again. As a child, I would have conversations with it all the time. I trusted it implicitly. I still remember having a slumber party with my best childhood friend less than a week before my mother passed away. At that time, there was no indication that her condition would deteriorate as quickly as it did. Yet I declared to my friend that my mother would leave us that week—three days later, she did. When my friend asked me how I had known this, I didn't quite have an explanation. *I just knew.*

Over the years, I lost touch with my inner voice. Like any friendship that is neglected, our relationship dwindled. Our darkest period was during college and the two years that followed graduation, but we rekindled our relationship the day I decided to leave my corporate job—and it's been getting stronger ever since. Today, I turn to my inner voice (my compass) all the time. There are still moments I choose to ignore it, because I'm not quite ready to deal with the consequences of what it's telling me, but I always promise to revisit the guidance at a later date.

## *HOW TO LOCATE YOUR INNER VOICE*

Everyone experiences their inner voice in a different way, but the most common places people locate it are in their head, heart, or gut (the area right behind your belly button). To find out if you're a head, heart, or gut person, start to pay attention to where you feel your body respond to an uncomfortable or exhilarating situation. Do you feel your chest constrict? Do you feel your stomach lurch? Do you feel nauseous? Do you start to have a conversation with yourself? Whatever it is, become acutely aware of the sensation and, instead of rejecting it, get curious about it: What is your body trying to tell you? Similarly, pay attention to when you *know* something with complete certainty. What does it feel like to *know it in your bones*?

## TURN UP THE VOLUME

If your purpose represents the highlighted route, your inner voice is your GPS. It's very similar to the maps application on your phone or the navigation system in your car, except without some of the system preferences. (Side note: Wouldn't it be great if we could select a specific accent and gender for our inner voice? Personally, I can't decide if I would prefer a smooth Morgan Freeman, hilarious Kristen Wiig, or wise Meryl Streep to guide me through life.) Lucky for you, the destination is already preprogrammed to your sweet spot—all you have to do is follow the route guidance. This isn't always as easy as it sounds, however. Most of us have unconsciously muted the volume on our GPS. We're essentially flying blind.

We are most connected to our inner voice when we're young. That's when the volume is at an all-time high. Children are naturally drawn to activities and environments that feel good and tend to avoid the situations that don't. They have yet to be polluted by societal norms, other people's opinions, man-made hierarchies, and the disease to please—just to name a few adult ills. As we grow up, through no fault of our own, we lose this blissful sense of ignorance. We discover that the fastest way to get what we want and to be acknowledged is to cater to those around us—even if it means silencing our inner voice. Over time, we become so accustomed to prioritizing other people's desires over our own that we can no longer distinguish one from the other.

While everyone conforms to some extent, women can be particularly sensitive to this type of pressure. We discount our own needs in order to satisfy other people's expectations. To lessen the discomfort or friction we may experience as a result, we tell ourselves stories: "My father sacrificed his dream of becoming a doctor, so I have to fulfill it for him." "I could never make money doing what I love." "People only respect me because of my hustle." These narratives are no more real than our favorite fairy tales, but they allow us to make sense of the world in the absence of an audible navigation system. Every time we tell or reinforce a story, we turn down the volume of our inner voice. Gradually, we become desensitized to what *actually* feels good to us and pursue exclusively what *looks* or *sounds* good to others. When we can't hear the route guidance from our GPS, we do what any well-intentioned, increasingly desperate driver would do: we follow the person in front of us. Surely, they know where they're going, right?

Not exactly. They might know where *they* are going, but their route isn't meant for you. No two people share the same highlighted route because no two people share the same purpose. Every individual has a unique cellular makeup—even identical twins don't have identical fingerprints. You have been blessed with a specific combination of life experiences, talents, sensitivities, fears, and desires. No one else shares your exact DNA. As a result, no one else on this planet is as qualified as you are to fulfill *your* purpose.

Now don't get me wrong, two people can absolutely share a *what* or *how*. There are millions of authors, nurses, needlepointers—you name the profession or passion. But each of these individuals is doing what they do for a different reason, albeit ever so slightly different. That's because each individual has a different sweet spot and is thus motivated by a different *why*. One author may write because she has a deep desire to share her expertise with those who need it, another author may write because it's the way he processes his own emotions, and a third author may write to honor the memory of a loved one.

In the absence of clear guidance, we are all trying to merge onto the same highlighted route. Because someone, somewhere, said that it was the right, smart, or respectful thing to do? Because following in someone else's footsteps feels easier than charting your own path? There are countless ways to justify this decision, but the inevitable result is a bumper-to-bumper traffic jam. You will find yourself caught behind millions of other vehicles, moving at a snail's pace for no good reason. No wonder you feel stuck, bored, and increasingly frustrated!

Fortunately, your inner voice isn't going anywhere. It will continue to direct you back to the highlighted route by giving you clues based on how you respond to certain activities, people, and places. You've simply conditioned yourself to ignore them. The solution to this predicament is obvious, of course: turn up the volume. You have to blast your inner voice so loud that you are afraid others might hear it. (Don't worry, I will be teaching you how to do this in the next chapter.)

This is no easy feat—especially if you've spent decades overriding your natural preferences. But with time and practice, you will become more aware of your inner voice and better versed in its preferred form of communication—until, eventually, you will no longer have to work so hard to hear it. From there, the next step is to learn to trust the voice, even when it gives you an answer you don't want to hear. Even when it forces you to admit that you aren't as happy as you're pretending to be, or that it's time to make some big, scary changes. Even when it means disappointing the people you love.

## ZIG WHEN OTHERS ZAG

As a little girl, I was a stereotypical Leo. (Yes, I'm referring to the astrological sign.) A personality test once described me as "bossy but caring," which pretty much sums me up perfectly. I knew what I wanted, wasn't afraid to speak my truth, had no problem ordering my siblings around, and thrived on being the center of attention.

I'm a proud Dutchie, and there are so many things I deeply appreciate about my heritage. The Dutch are kind, conscious citizens, with an insatiable sense for adventure. They are decidedly inclusive and always (*always*) give it to you straight. Sugarcoating is not part of the Dutch vocabulary. Growing up, however, I always felt like the odd one out. Why? The reason is perhaps best illustrated by a famous Dutch saying, loosely translated: "Just be normal, that's crazy enough." This mentality is deeply ingrained in our culture. You're encouraged to keep your head down, go with the flow, and whatever you do, *don't* stand out from the crowd.

You can imagine how my fiery Leo self struggled to fit in. My family was not surprised when, at age eleven, I announced I was going to study in America. While it wasn't completely out of left field, it was certainly different. To give you a sense, I only knew two or three others in my whole school district who were applying to American universities. This isn't shocking, given that student life in Holland is notoriously fun and costs a small fraction of the amount required to attend a university overseas.

I share this story because it represents the last time in a long time I zigged when others zagged. As I started my new life in the States, I lost touch with my inner voice and the young girl who fearlessly followed her heart, spoke her truth, and danced around the kitchen dreaming of being world famous one day. I started to adapt. I started to "tone it down." So much so that many of my college friends wouldn't recognize the young girl who so readily commanded the spotlight.

Does this sound familiar? You may not have aspired to center stage, but are there dreams you gave up on or personality traits you tempered in order to appease others? In what ways have you consciously or unconsciously dimmed your own light?

## FOLLOW YOUR HELL YESES

Even now, it can be difficult for me to discern whether I'm being honest with myself. Am I doing something because I *want* to, or because I know it will result in the least amount of friction for myself and others? Whenever I suspect the latter might be at play, I do the following exercise:

1. **Think about the decision you have to make.** Close your eyes and visualize your decision tree—the various ways you might choose to respond or act.

2. **Play out each potential scenario in your mind.** Put yourself in the shoes of the future you who is living with that new reality.

3. **Pay attention to how each scenario feels in your body.** Does it feel icky? Do you feel guilty? Or is it a *hell yes*? Go with the option that feels the closest to the latter.

Trusting your inner voice takes courage. It requires you to venture beyond your comfort zone and question the stories you've come to view as truths. It requires you to let go of the person you so badly *want* other people to see. It requires you to express your desires and confront any resistance that is standing in your way. Most of all, however, it requires you to take responsibility. Responsibility for your choices about how you spend your time, who you surround yourself with, and how you show up for the people and projects you're invested in. It is not your job to worry about what other people might think of your actions. Because at the end of the day, despite what you tell yourself, you have zero control over how they respond. It *is* your job, however, to listen to what lights you up and follow that spark, wherever it might take you.

You're already well on your way. Purchasing this book was most likely a response to a nudge from your inner voice. Whether it was a gentle whisper or a deafening scream, the guidance was clear: "Please take a U-turn."

# CHAPTER FOUR

# PREPARE FOR TAKEOFF

*"No one ever made a difference by
being like everyone else."*
—P.T. Barnum

You are about to embark on a series of "Discovery Missions." These missions come in the form of questions, and each prompt is designed to uncover a little more about your most authentic self.

You may have answered some of these questions before, but I can guarantee you that you've never answered them all at once, or in this sequence. Over the years, we've refined the prompts to be as concise but comprehensive as possible. Each was selected to give you important insights into one or more of the circles from the sweet spot framework: your passions, your strengths, and your potential to contribute. This method has been tested with hundreds of students, so before you come up with a million reasons this process *won't* work, try to suspend your judgment and approach the exercise with a sense of openness.

I purposefully didn't say "open mind" because the key to completing these missions successfully is to take your mind out of the equation entirely. It's about getting out of your head and into your body so you can tune into your inner voice and channel it onto the page. At the risk of losing any skeptics to the word "channel," I am going to make this as prescriptive as possible by sharing some ground rules. If you follow these rules, I guarantee the channeling will feel almost effortless—perhaps even enjoyable.

Here are the ground rules.

## 1. DO NOT SELF-EDIT.

It sounds obvious, but most of us have been programmed to self-edit from a very young age. As infants, we are still permitted to show up as our full, unapologetic selves. Whether we're hungry, scared, frustrated, or happy, there's no hiding how we feel about things. Toddlers are notorious for blurting out the truth with no regard for how it might affect those around them—often to the grave embarrassment of their parents. From that point on, however, we start to learn the art of self-censorship. As our speech and social skills develop, so does our ability to discern what is or isn't "appropriate" to say in public. We learn to think before we speak, and soon it becomes second nature.

While self-editing may indeed reduce friction in our daily lives, I always find it refreshing to be around people who have a limited amount of conditioning in this department. Take my childhood friend Laura, for example. Laura was one of the first friends I made in elementary school after moving to the Netherlands from the United Kingdom in first grade. Fortunately for me, she embraced my lanky limbs and unusual accent with open arms. As an outsider, I felt instantly drawn to her. Whatever Dutch DNA I lacked, Laura had in spades. She was tall with white-blonde hair and blue eyes. She was also the most direct and sincere person I have ever met. She always says exactly what's on her mind—for better and for worse. (Bless her parents for encouraging instead of squashing this personality trait.)

On my first day back at school after my mother passed away, our fifth grade teacher gathered the class together in a circle. I'm not sure exactly how she envisioned this going—it was likely the first time a student of hers had lost a parent—but she asked if anyone had a question for me. When Laura's hand shot up, I was surprised to say the least. Not by the fact that someone dared to ask a question in this uncomfortable situation, but because it was *Laura*, one of my closest friends. She could have easily waited for a more private setting like recess. I braced myself. True to her nature and without hesitation, Laura asked: "So who's going to be your new mom now?" The teacher turned bright red and instantly realized what a bad idea this had been. I can't remember exactly how I answered the question, but to this day I still tease Laura about it. But teasing aside, it's one of my favorite qualities in her. It reminds me how most adults tend to overcomplicate things by dancing around the issue or the question in an attempt not to ruffle any feathers. I bet Laura wasn't the only classmate that day wondering who my new mom would be, but she was the only one who was unencumbered enough to ask.

Of course, there are many situations in which self-editing is the right thing to do. Finding your purpose is not one of them, however. For this process to work, you have to channel your inner Laura and trust the first answer that comes to mind. This is not about writing down the response you think you *should*, or the one you most want others to hear. It's about discovering *your* truth. No one else is going to read your answers (unless you want them to), so there is absolutely no reason *not* to be 100 percent honest with yourself. If you do self-edit, you might as well skip this entire section because the purpose you end up with will not be authentic.

## 2. SET A TIME LIMIT.

One of the most effective ways to increase creativity is to impose limitations. It sounds counterintuitive, but the more restricted you are, the more inclined you'll be to push creative boundaries. Jazz musicians use this technique when improvising. While it can appear like they have no idea what note will come next, they're actually abiding by a strict set of rules. Similarly, if you've ever been to an improv comedy show, you will notice that most of the skits require input from the audience, thereby limiting the creative liberties of the cast. Without audience input, the sheer number of options would be too overwhelming for the comedians to produce anything worthwhile, let alone laugh-out-loud funny.

The famous composer Igor Stravinsky was renowned for his love of constraints: "My freedom will be so much greater and more meaningful the more narrowly I limit my field of action and the more I surround myself with obstacles." Inspired by some of his favorite classical composers, Stravinsky would assign similarly strict guardrails to his own creative process. He believed this would only enhance his work as it would require more resourcefulness and imagination to create something truly original.

As you embark on your Discovery Missions in the next chapter, I am going to ask you to time yourself. You will have two minutes to respond to each question, and it's imperative you hold yourself to that. You can use a kitchen timer or the stopwatch on your smartphone—whatever does the trick. The reason I am imposing this limitation on you is because these are big, juicy questions. Without any restrictions, you might find yourself writing for hours on end. By adding a timer, you will be forced to get straight to the heart of the matter. It will prevent you from self-editing as you go because you don't have a second to waste. Furthermore, it will encourage you to venture beyond the stories you've adopted to discover your own original truth, just like Stravinsky did.

## 3. USE A PEN AND PAPER.

For some of you, I might as well be asking you to use a quill, but hear me out. There is quite a bit of scientific evidence that suggests that writing things down the good old-fashioned way not only enables you to process the information better, but also allows you to tap into your subconscious more easily. The repetitive motion of writing creates an almost meditative state, so you can more easily connect to your inner voice without getting distracted by the desire to paint a pretty picture.

Whether you use a journal, a notepad, or printer paper for this part of the process is entirely up to you. A little later in the book we will start to make sense of the madness, and I will offer helpful templates to summarize and organize your thoughts. For now, just use whatever writing tools are available to you, but make sure you have plenty of pages to work with.

## 4. DO NOT EMBELLISH.

Your inner voice is surprisingly succinct. It often comes through in a single word or a short, pithy paragraph. As you start to tap into your inner well of wisdom, don't feel the need to write full, cohesive, or even grammatically correct sentences. Just make it legible enough for you to decipher afterward.

Try to think of yourself as a stenographer. (This is the person who sits in the corner of a court room taking copious notes and is responsible for preparing the official hearing transcripts.) During the Discovery Missions, you are simply transcribing what your inner voice is telling you. Take your opinions and your judgments out of it—there will be plenty of time to reflect on your responses afterward. Just write down exactly what you hear—no more, no less.

## 5. SET THE MOOD.

It's important that you create a space where you can get quiet enough to hear the answers. Don't do this exercise with kids playing in the background, in between meetings, or when you're expecting a phone call. Be intentional about choosing a time and place where you can focus, without interruption, on tuning in to what your inner voice is trying to communicate to you. Ask your partner to take the kids outside, block off the morning on your calendar, or take yourself out on a date to your favorite coffee shop, park, or reading nook in your house.

Whatever you do, don't feel guilty about indulging in your personal development. View it as a gift to yourself, as well as those around you. As every frequent flyer knows, you have to put your own oxygen mask on first *before* you can show up to support others. Surround yourself with things that inspire or delight you, whether it's a cappuccino, a view of the ocean, or your favorite playlist. Don't rush the process and make it as enjoyable as you possibly can. This is supposed to be fun!

Finally, try to complete all the Discovery Missions in one sitting. Because it's timed, this should take no more than forty-five minutes (depending on how much time you need in between each question to reset). Completing the missions in one sitting will enable you to get in a flow state, which is where the real magic happens. What is a flow state? It's a state of mind that allows you to lose track of time. You will put pen to paper and your hand will effortlessly start to scribble. It will feel like you're *allowing* the answers to come through, instead of forcing them to. If you follow the previous ground rules, you should be able to access this state of mind after a question or two.

# CHAPTER FIVE

# YOUR DISCOVERY MISSIONS

Your turn. Remember the ground rules and reset your timer for two minutes after completing each mission. Try to avoid looking ahead at the questions to come—the less prepared you feel, the better. If you finish writing before the timer goes, that's okay. However, I encourage you to try keeping your pen to paper for the entire two minutes, even if you find yourself going on a tangent. You never know where these side roads may lead, after all. Feel free to stretch and shake out your hand if it's getting tired, but I recommend limiting your breaks to in between questions. The name of the game is to just keep writing.

I recommend copying each question or mission first before answering it. Now grab your pen and paper, set your timer, and let's do this.

**Discovery Mission #1**
I am at my best when:

**Discovery Mission #2**
I am at my worst when:

**Discovery Mission #3**
People often compliment me on my:

**Discovery Mission #4**

People often come to me for:

**Discovery Mission #5**

If you had unlimited resources and knew you could not fail, what would you choose to do?

**Discovery Mission #6**

What events or people have had a profound impact on the way you see the world and your values?

**Discovery Mission #7**

Imagine your eightieth birthday party. You are happy and fulfilled. Someone gets up to toast you. What would you like them to say about your life?

**Discovery Mission #8**

Given your unique strengths and values, what are your most meaningful contributions to the important people in your life? What are your superpowers?

**Discovery Mission #9**

What things do you feel you should do or change, even if you may have dismissed these thoughts many times?

**Discovery Mission #10**

What did you love to do as a child? What activities make you lose track of time today?

**Discovery Mission #11**

Who are you envious of? What do you secretly want that they have?

**Discovery Mission #12**

What personal accomplishment(s) are you most proud of?

Congrats. You did it! That wasn't as painful as you thought it would be, right? Hopefully it was even enjoyable at times.

If you're anything like me, your hand is probably throbbing by now as it's no longer used to writing for long periods of time. Fortunately, the exercises in chapters 6 and 7 require very little (if any) writing on your part. In fact, it will feel more like an arts and crafts project than anything else. While I encourage you to maintain this momentum, now is a good time to take a little breather if you need it. Refill your coffee mug, walk around the block, or do some desk yoga. Try to stay in your personal bubble, however, and avoid social media or other people if possible.

# CHAPTER SIX

# *YOUR PURPOSE TRIGGERS*

In order to live on purpose, you have to know your purpose. As I mentioned earlier, however, your purpose is not *one* thing—nor is it constant. Your purpose is whatever makes you come alive. As such, "finding your purpose" is the act of identifying what makes you come alive.

We are constantly surrounded by clues reminding us what our purpose is—we simply don't know where to look. We are so stuck in our own narrative and the traps of what we "should" be doing that we overlook the obvious. The Discovery Missions were designed to get you out of this broken operating system and into a flow state so you can momentarily suspend judgment. Now that you've collected the various data points from your subconscious, it's time to search for clues. I call these clues Purpose Triggers:

> A Purpose Trigger is an activity, person, environment, or feeling that gives you a heightened sense of meaning.

It's something that occurs in your daily life that sets your soul on fire and brings you pure, unadulterated joy. It makes you feel as if you're exactly where you're supposed to be, doing exactly what you were born to do.

Grab a highlighter or a different-colored pen and take about ten to fifteen minutes to read through your responses to the Discovery Missions. Pay close attention to recurring themes or patterns and highlight or underline these patterns as you go. Think of yourself as a detective investigating a case. You're looking for any insights or data points that might connect one event or character to another. Like any good detective, it's important to stay objective. In fact, it might help to pretend that the responses are someone else's entirely. As you review the words on the page, ask yourself, what stands out? Are there particular people, personality traits, places, or talents that continue to come up? For example, you might notice that many of the answers refer to outdoor activities, or perhaps there is a common theme of serving others. Whatever it is, do not question, judge, or analyze it (yet). Simply circle, highlight, or underline the key words.

Return to this page when you're done.

## DEFINE YOUR PURPOSE TRIGGERS

The next step is to turn the underlined or highlighted words into Purpose Triggers: specific activities, people, environments, and feelings that light you up and make you feel like your best, most fulfilled self. Things that remind you of your why, your sweet spot.

I'll give you an example from my own purpose journey:

One of my favorite pastimes as a child was playing an imaginary game I called "Classroom." As you might have guessed, I was the teacher and would coerce my poor siblings and their unsuspecting friends to volunteer as student tributes. I took my responsibilities *very* seriously. I would carefully plan my lessons in advance, assign homework, conduct pop quizzes, and score each one meticulously—even handing out gold stars to top students. (If any of my former "students" are reading this, please accept my sincerest apologies for any permanent damage I may have done.) Until I embarked on my Discovery Missions, I had forgotten all about my former "career" as a school teacher.

Then, about two years ago, I felt a calling to sign up for a local yoga teacher training. I had convinced myself that I was drawn to the course because of a desire to deepen my yoga practice and build a local community, as I was new to town. It never occurred to me that I might actually want to teach by the end of it. But as soon as the training started, it became clear as day. The process of guiding students through a sixty-minute class—from choosing a theme to creating a playlist and designing a sequence of postures—gave me the same rush I had experienced in my make-believe classroom. Something about curating a space where my students can learn to see and embody their full potential—on as well as off the mat—is extremely rewarding to me.

The final clue became evident when reflecting on my response to Discovery Mission #11: *What personal accomplishment(s) are you most proud of?* One of the achievements I listed was developing the Find Your Purpose workshop—the curriculum that ultimately inspired this book. Turning my own revelations about designing a life on purpose into a structured process that can help *others* achieve the same result is by far one of the most impactful things I have done to date.

On their own, each of these data points may seem insignificant. But when I reviewed my responses through an objective detective's lens, they became neon signs pointing toward one of my most powerful Purpose Triggers today: teaching and developing others.

In our workshops, the Purpose Triggers that come up are all over the map. No two people describe the same combination of triggers, even if they share one or two in common. One young man discovered that his most poignant trigger was creating music—yet he hadn't picked up his guitar in years. Another woman noticed that she was happiest when hosting groups or individuals in her home, but she had never viewed this with any particular regard. A third student observed a pattern of community building, which encouraged her to explore a whole new category of job opportunities and build a personal brand around this previously underacknowledged talent.

Now it's your turn. Come up with three to five Purpose Triggers of your own based on the patterns and themes you discovered in the previous exercise. I am purposefully (pun intended) not including a list of triggers for you to choose from. While the aforementioned examples may resonate with you to some degree, it's important that you stay true to what came up during your own Discovery Missions. Remember, this isn't about what you *should* enjoy or excel at—it's about being courageous enough to allow your true self to shine through.

## My Purpose Triggers

1. _____
2. _____
3. _____
4. _____
5. _____

# THE POWER OF CURIOSITY

A Purpose Trigger can often come disguised as a curiosity. Just as you have to learn to trust your inner voice, you have to learn to trust your curiosities. They are important signs along the path to your sweet spot. When I first started listening to Oprah's *SuperSoul Conversations* podcast, I never imagined it would lead me to writing a book one day. I was just curious about how other people had discovered their purpose and what strategies had been successful for them. Soon, I was hooked—I consumed any self-help book, personality test, podcast, or TED Talk I could find. One thing continued to lead to another and now here we are.

If you're struggling to pinpoint your Purpose Triggers, start by asking yourself the question: What am I most curious about?

## CREATE ALIGNMENT

Now that you've suspended judgment long enough to identify your Purpose Triggers, it's time to determine whether your current reality is setting you up for a purpose-driven life.

Head to www.purposeplaybook.com/alignmentplanner to download the PDF planner exercise. Use a blank planner page to describe a typical day in your life. Be honest—and if you find yourself struggling because every day is so different, simply start by describing yesterday. Be as specific and detailed as possible. For example, you might want to include time spent on activities such as returning emails, meeting with direct reports, volunteering at school, doing laundry, working out, playing with kids, date night, reading before bed, coffee with a friend, morning meditation, etc.

Once you have filled out the planner page, compare and contrast your typical day to your list of Purpose Triggers: *How much of your time and energy is dedicated to the activities, people, environments, or feelings that bring you joy?* The downloadable will help you calculate the exact percentage of your waking hours that are spent on activities that align with your Purpose Triggers. Then consider how that time is divided up across your different Purpose Triggers. Perhaps you are doing very well at prioritizing one of your triggers while completely neglecting another, for example.

This is not meant to be a punitive exercise, so don't get discouraged if the percentage is low or if the distribution is uneven. This is simply meant to give you a concrete number to reflect on so you can determine where you might have room to improve. Next, brainstorm small, incremental changes you can make that will allow you to incorporate more triggers into your day-to-day. Outsourcing some of the activities that don't align with your triggers or setting better boundaries are both excellent ways to free up more time for the things that bring you joy. Here are a few examples of small changes past workshop participants have made to achieve better alignment:

Ordering groceries online

Hiring a virtual assistant

Declining invitations to volunteer at school

Implementing a personal policy of no work calls after
5:00 p.m.

Keeping phone on airplane mode until 8:00 a.m.

**To get you started, complete the following sentences:**

To better align my time with my Purpose Triggers,
I am going to:

**STOP** _____

**CONTINUE** _____

**START** _____

**Here's how I might fill this out:**

To better align my time with my Purpose Triggers,
I am going to:

**STOP** browsing Instagram for thirty minutes before bed, so I can read or spend quality time with my
husband instead

**CONTINUE** moving my body daily by doing yoga
or getting into nature

**START** my day off more slowly and avoid checking email until 8:00 a.m.

There is no need to forcibly incorporate every one of your Purpose Triggers into an already packed schedule. One hundred percent alignment is impossible, so be gracious with yourself. It is also important to be mindful of the natural ebb and flow of life, and how this might impact your alignment over time. Depending on the season you're in, it may make more sense to prioritize certain triggers over others, so be strategic. It will also vary from person to person. For example, the summer might be a great time for *me* to learn a new skill because many of our clients are out of the office; however, if you're a parent, the summer may be the worst possible time to start something because your kids are home from school.

The point of this exercise is to get you off autopilot so you can bring more awareness to how you spend your time and energy. The goal is to identify opportunities to infuse your daily grind with a little more purpose. The bottom line is that you should be filling your calendar with things that fill your plate.

# CHAPTER SEVEN

# YOUR PURPOSE STATEMENT

Remember the Howard Thurman quote? "Do not ask what the world needs. Ask yourself what makes you come alive, because what the world needs is people who have come alive."

Well, your Purpose Statement is meant to encapsulate exactly that: *what makes you come alive.* Your *why.* Your reason for being—or raison d'être, as the French call it. It reflects you as your most fulfilled self, when you're living in alignment with your Purpose Triggers and operating in your sweet spot: where your strengths, passions, and potential to contribute collide.

Why create a Purpose Statement? Because there's a lot of value in putting your purpose into words. Research shows that people who take the time to write down their goals are significantly more likely to achieve said goals.[7] Not only does it help you internalize the objective, but it also provides a sense of accountability. The same holds true for your purpose—and it can be a particularly important exercise given how ethereal the concept often feels to people. By articulating your purpose in a single, memorable sentence, you make it concrete. This also allows you to refer back to your statement frequently. You want this sentence to resonate with you, to keep echoing in your brain so it can shape your daily decisions. Whenever you find yourself at a crossroads or have an important decision to make, you can use your statement as a filter by asking yourself, which of these choices or actions are most aligned with my Purpose Statement?

There are two options for crafting your Purpose Statement: freestyle or guided. Before you get started, however, I want to go over a few important guidelines:

1. **Your Purpose Statement puts your sweet spot into words.** It should describe you as your best, thriving self: where your passions, strengths, and potential to contribute intersect. It can be helpful to refer back to your Purpose Triggers for this exercise, but don't feel the need to list *all* your triggers.

2. **Your Purpose Statement does *not* need to reflect your reality today**. You just started this journey, so there's a good chance that your day-to-day life does not align perfectly with your Purpose Triggers *yet*. Don't be intimidated or dissuaded. In fact, your Purpose Statement should be equal parts inspirational and *aspirational*. It's meant to give you room to grow.

3. **Your Purpose Statement is a work in progress.** Because purpose is not a final destination, your statement can be ever-evolving. Don't put too much pressure on yourself to make it perfect from the outset. You can (and will) continue to tweak your Purpose Statement.

See this as a first draft and prepare for a lifetime of editing.

4. **Your Purpose Statement is 100 percent for you**. You're not writing a Twitter bio or a LinkedIn description. This sentence is meant to inspire you and only you.

5. **Your Purpose Statement is most powerful when internalized.** Once you've crafted your Purpose Statement, remember to refer back to it often. Print it out or write it on a sticky note and place it in various places throughout your home or office.

If you started sweating when you read "freestyle," you can opt for a guided approach using the Purpose Statement Builder in this chapter. If you would like a printable version, go to www.purpose-playbook.com/statementbuilder to access your free template. Remember that this is just meant to be a guide—you are welcome to move around the blanks or substitute words to make it work for you. The template is a tool to help get you started, but it is by no means the only approach to crafting your statement.

### Purpose Statement Builder Template

My purpose in life is to light myself up by [*insert Purpose Trigger(s)*] so that I can show up as my best self and contribute to the world around me by [*insert potential to contribution and/or impact you want to have*].

If you're having trouble conceptualizing what a Purpose Statement is, here are a few examples using our Purpose Statement Builder:

My purpose in life is to light myself up by spending time in nature, so that I can show up as my best self and contribute to the world around me by encouraging people to be more conscious about the decisions they make and the products they consume.

My purpose in life is to light myself up by seeking out opportunities to travel and meet new people, so that I can show up as my best self and share these stories and experiences with others through my writing and photography.

My purpose in life is to light myself up by creating a beautiful and safe environment for my family, so that I can show up as my best self and raise the next generation of strong, loving, and conscious leaders.

My purpose in life is to light myself up by learning new things and exploring the mysteries of life, so that I can show up as my best self and contribute to the world around me by translating this wisdom in a relatable, engaging way for others.

My purpose in life is to light myself up by surround-

ing myself with beautiful things and giving myself the
space to create, so that I inspire others with my art.

If you're a creative soul at heart or happen to have a knack for
putting feelings into words, you may want to take a freestyle approach. Don't let yourself be limited by a formula and take full creative liberty in drafting your own Purpose Statement. My only recommendation is that you try and keep it to a single sentence—not
a ten-page manifesto.

## SWEET SPOT MAPPING

A helpful way to kick-start the brainstorm for your Purpose
Statement is to create a mind map. A mind map is often
used to generate new ideas, visualize your thoughts, and
organize them around key themes. Here's how it works:

**Step 1.** Get three blank pieces of paper, one for each of the
three categories of the sweet spot framework: Passions,
Strengths, and Contributions. Write the category name in
the center of the piece of paper and draw a circle around it so
it looks like a bubble.

**Step 2.** Starting with one of the categories, write down any
related words that come to mind. For example, if one of
your passions is music, you will draw a line coming out of
the "Passions" bubble in the center of your paper and write
"Music." Then continue to draw lines coming out of the
"Music" bubble featuring all the words that come to mind
when you think of music: my guitar, Spotify, live concerts,
etc. By connecting each new word to its respective category

with a line, the bubbles will start to look like hubs with a myriad of spokes.

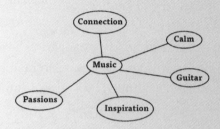

**Step 3.** Continue this process for each passion that comes to mind. Instead of exclusively focusing on things, try to include feelings and emotions you associate with the word. Keep going until you can't think of anything else to add. For example:

Passions

       Music

              Guitar
              Calm
              Inspiration
              Connection

**Step 4.** Repeat this process for the remaining categories.

**Step 5.** Reflect on your mind map and the connections between certain activities and feelings or emotions. Use these insights to fill in the blanks of your Purpose Statement.

# VISUALIZATION EXERCISE: A DAY IN YOUR DREAM LIFE

Visualization can be a very powerful tool on your journey to purpose. It can allow you to experience what life will be like if you continue to listen to your inner voice and take the required actions to achieve greater alignment with your Purpose Triggers. Painting a picture of your future reality will not only give you greater clarity about where you're headed, but it will also give you the confidence to overcome roadblocks along the way. By creating a vivid image in your mind, you can continue to remind yourself why you're on this path to begin with.

Grab a journal or a piece of paper and write a paragraph about what life will be like when you are living *on purpose*. Describe a day in your purpose-driven life: How do you feel when you wake up? How do you spend your day and how does it make you feel? Who are you surrounding yourself with? Where are you living? Include as much detail as you can.

PART THREE

# LIVE ON PURPOSE

# CHAPTER EIGHT

# READY. SET. PURPOSE.

> "Instead of trying to think your way into
> a new way of action, it's time to act your
> way into a new way of thinking."
> —Jerry Sternin, director of the
> Positive Deviance Initiative

Take a moment to congratulate yourself, because you have successfully (re)discovered and articulated your purpose!

I wish I could tell you that the hard work is done, but the fact of the matter is that it's really just beginning. Identifying your purpose is one thing—a thing to be proud of, no doubt—but *acting* on that information is a whole new ball game. Yet without action, your Purpose Statement will remain a collection of meaningless words. Now that you know better—now that you know what it will take for you to thrive—abandoning the highlighted route will be all the more disappointing.

## INTENTION + ACTION = RESULTS

Connecting intention to action is hard. A good intention, albeit honorable, is not enough to live on purpose. Action is ultimately what stands in between your current potential and your reality; it's what separates those who thrive from those who survive—and you haven't come this far to go back to surviving.

This feels like a good time to practice some tough love and remind you that there is only one person behind the wheel—one person who is ultimately responsible for the outcome of your journey. If there's any doubt as to who that person is, take a long, hard look in the mirror. I know for a fact that this formula works, but it doesn't matter how well I break down each step or how carefully you read the pages that follow; you will *only* succeed if you trust the process and if you're willing to do the work, no matter what stories you must rewrite or resistance you must overcome. Remember that you are in control of your attitude and your actions. At any given point, you can navigate back to the highlighted route and start living the life you were destined to. And if you don't for some reason—if you choose to take another (less fulfilling) route—*it's on you*. It's not on me, your parents, your coworkers, your partner, your therapist, or your kids. The buck stops with you. Part Three is where the rubber meets the road, so it's time to cut the crap and stop being a passenger in your own life.

## ONE STEP AT A TIME

Are there certain accomplishments that you admire in others but believe in your heart of hearts you will *never* make yourself? Perhaps you don't believe you physically *can* do it, or maybe you have absolutely no desire to—or both? Despite knowing better, my list of "nevers" is quite long. Number one is bungee jumping. Number two is running a marathon. Number three is having more than five kids. Number four, until a few months ago, was writing a book. I always *enjoyed* writing, but I couldn't imagine actually sitting down to write a full manuscript—not to mention build a personal platform to promote the book (which is still the most intimidating part for me). On top of that, I highly doubted that anyone would be interested in reading 200 pages of my word vomit— even those who love me most. I have several friends who have either written or plan to write a book, and I was always the first to respond that "I could never do it." I meant it too. So no one was more surprised than I was when I declared my dream of becoming a published author.

It was December 2018. Out of nowhere, my inner voice came through loud and clear: *you have to write a book about finding your purpose.* It took me several weeks to start paying attention to this thought, but by January 1st the intention had comfortably nestled itself in my conscience. As I shared earlier, however, an intention means very little if it isn't paired with action. I knew I could easily continue to live with this secret desire and come up with excuses not to start: no time, no point, too much money. Moreover, my inner critic was all over this idea: Who do you think you are? What do you have to say that hasn't already been said before by *real* authors? What are your friends and family going to think when they read it?

Despite my doubts and excuses, I kept moving forward—I kept taking action. It was nothing major at first. I created a new document on my laptop and started working on an outline. Every few days, I would sit down, pick a section, and write for an hour or two. Some weeks, I would make time in the mornings before the daily email tsunami ensued; other weeks, I would spend an entire Saturday ensconced on the couch. By the end of January, I had about eighty pages, but I still hadn't told anyone what I was working on—partially because I was afraid of what they would say, but mostly because I didn't want to put any unnecessary pressure on myself. I soon realized, however, that if I truly believed in this book, I had to establish some form of accountability—some way to ensure that I didn't let my inner critic win. So I told my husband and my business partner what I was doing. To my surprise, they seemed to genuinely support the idea—so I kept writing. Now that I had expressed my desire out loud, I did feel more pressure to make progress, but I was ready for it now; I had incubated the idea long enough to know there was something worth fighting for. Then, when I started to get close to a final rough draft, I hired an editor. It felt a little self-indulgent—editors are for *real* writers, after all—but it was one more person who could hold me accountable. If I was going to do this, I had to go all in.

During the six months it took me to complete my first draft, I faced every possible variation of imposter syndrome. Every time I heard about another influencer publishing a self-help book, I would wonder why I even bothered. Every time a new client project would come up, I'd abandon my manuscript and consider never opening it again. Every time my husband offered me some constructive criticism, I threatened to throw in the towel. But I didn't. I kept putting one foot in front of the other. I kept taking one small action at a time. I kept choosing to live on purpose. Instead of letting the grand vision of publishing a book get the best of me—I didn't actually start referring to it as a "book" until I got an editor, mind you—I focused on the next best step. In all honesty, what motivated me to keep going was how much I enjoyed it. Writing this book became one of my greatest Purpose Triggers. When I sat down to write, I would lose track of time. It was my happy place. Contrary to what I had pictured this process looking like just a few months prior, I now looked forward to waking up early and locking myself in my home office all weekend. It was no longer just about the outcome—I didn't care whether the book would be read by one person or one million people. All I cared about was getting to write. All I had to do was get out of my own way and give myself permission to lean into the pull.

I will admit that this book is an exception. I have had countless intentions that never manifested, and I wanted some of those things just as badly as I wanted this book. The big difference is that, in this case, I took action. When I encountered a roadblock or found myself on a detour, I did whatever I needed to in order to reconnect with my internal compass—I turned up the volume—and made my way back to the highlighted route.

While I cannot do the work for you, I *can* set you up for success by sharing some of the lessons I've learned along the way. In the next few chapters, I will help you anticipate and avoid several of the most common pitfalls people encounter on their path to purpose. I call these obstacles "Purpose Blockers." I will also offer some helpful strategies that will enable you to take continuous, inspired action toward your purpose. These are your "Purpose Enablers."

# CHAPTER NINE

# PURPOSE BLOCKERS

A Purpose Blocker is something that attempts to lure you off your highlighted route. What's especially tricky is that they often come disguised in the form of a perfectly legitimate excuse or story: "I can't pursue my purpose because my kids need me at home right now." "I can't pursue my purpose because there are too many other people doing what I want to do already." Or, "I can't pursue my purpose because it would be a waste of my education." On the surface, these sound like valid reasons to put your purpose on hold, but the fix is temporary. While these excuses may silence your discomfort in the short term, they do so at the expense of your long-term fulfillment. Living on purpose means embracing your truest self, and the sooner you can do this, the sooner you can start contributing in a meaningful way to those around you. Using your kids as a decoy or comparing yourself to others is shortsighted at best. Would you rather start living on purpose *today* or spend the next few decades doing "fine"—until you finally run out of excuses?

There are infinite variations of Purpose Blockers, and you may be more sensitive to some than others. I will explore the six blockers that I believe to be the most universal and expose them for what they really are. I will also share some of the tactics I use to protect myself from these blockers, so you always have a trick or two up your sleeve. No worthwhile pursuit is without obstacles. The key is to cultivate enough self-awareness to recognize these speed bumps when they arise and address them head-on, before they can do any serious damage.

## *PURPOSE BLOCKER #1*
### CRITICS: HATERS GONNA HATE

*"The loudest boos always come from the cheapest seats."*
—Babe Ruth

On the whole, I believe the benefits of social media outweigh the negatives. Social media has enabled me to stalk my high school friends halfway across the world; stay on top of major life events like engagements, weddings, and babies; and given me access to an endless feed (literally) of inspiration, including bucket-list destinations, recipes, and motivational quotes. For that, I am very grateful.

But, of course, I am not blind to the dark side of social media.

In a world where people can hide behind a mobile device and a fake profile picture, it's hard (nay, impossible) to block out the haters. While we know deep down that their commentary is driven by insecurity and a sense of lack in their own lives, it doesn't make the words less hurtful. On top of that, the more authentically you show up and share your voice, the louder the boos seem to become. In this environment, it can be tempting to filter your true self in order to appease and appeal to these trolls . . . but does that mean you should? Absolutely not.

Sadly, this doesn't just apply to social media—trolls exist outside the social spheres too. And they don't just prey on individuals. If you want to see some of the most egregious trolling in action, consider what corporations have to deal with on a daily basis.

I remember receiving a call from one of our clients who worked in the marketing department of a top US retail bank. He called to ask for our advice. The bank, known for its commitment to diversity and inclusion, had recently taken a bold stance in a national advertising campaign featuring a same-sex couple. (I hope one day the fact that this was a "bold" move will seem unimaginable.) Our client was calling because the bank had started to receive public scrutiny from an important shareholder who disagreed with what the ad implied. The shareholder was threatening to cut ties with the bank if they continued to run the campaign. The bank was forced to choose between staying true to its values—the principles it openly (and passionately) preached to its employees and customers—and giving in to a bully. In this case, the bully was just *one* person and a handful of his cowardly followers, but he had significant leverage over the bank. Our inclination as humans is to zero in on the *one* negative comment or voice in the room while overlooking the sea of nodding heads. In fact, humans are wired to remember negative emotions more vividly than positive emotions. For example, studies have found that it takes five positive events to make up for a single negative one.[8]

Fortunately, the bank decided to keep running the ad, and I have never been more proud to call them a client. This was exactly why we created our company in the first place: to show the world's most powerful and resource-rich corporations that these decisions *matter*. That how they respond to a situation like this can guarantee their success or demise decades from now. That they are setting an example and thereby establishing a new standard. Our client raised the bar that day for banks and companies everywhere by making a statement: bullies cannot and will not deter us from acting in alignment with our purpose. Now that's a company I would bet on.

So, if this multibillion-dollar bank was able to ignore the haters with the eyes of the world on them—including one of their biggest shareholders—surely we can muster up the courage to stay grounded in our own worth and stand up against our own bullies.

You will never be able to please or appeal to everyone. The sooner you can accept this truth, the easier it will become. It can be excruciatingly hard at first, but I promise that if you continue to show up as your true self, you will eventually hit a tipping point. At first, your haters will grow in proportion to your authenticity. But, as time goes on, they will dwindle. As soon as they realize that you are steadfastly committed to your why, you become a lot less interesting to them, and they will promptly find a new victim to take out their insecurities on.

## *PURPOSE PLAYS:*
### TACTICS TO IGNORE THE BOOS

Your best defense against haters is to keep your eyes on the prize: the highlighted route in front of you. Double down on your purpose and channel whatever emotions they evoke inside of you toward something more productive.

If you're still struggling to drown out the negative noise, here are some tactics to consider:

1. **Remind yourself that it's not about *you*.** Robin Sharma said it best: "Other people's opinions of you are none of your business." The fact that they need to make you feel small to empower themselves has absolutely nothing to do with you and everything to do with them and their own baggage.

2. **Send them some love.** They clearly need it. I'm not suggesting that you acknowledge their mean comment with a heart emoji or dignify a hateful message with a response. All I'm suggesting is that you practice empathy. Imagine what type of crappy situation they must be going through or how boring and unfulfilling their life must be to want to waste their time on trolling. Then send a little love or positivity their way. I promise it will make you feel better too.

3. **Lift someone else up.** It sounds simple, but it's surprisingly effective. Karma is a real thing: you receive in proportion to what you give.

4. **Focus on your fans.** I am willing to bet that for every person who tries to bring you down, there are at least five or more people waiting in line to lift you up and sing your praises. Instead of wasting your energy on the haters, redirect your attention to the people who deserve it most. Allow yourself to accept their compliments and words of affirmation, rather than brushing them

off. Create a mental or digital file with your fan mail, so you can revisit it whenever you need a little confidence boost.

# PURPOSE BLOCKER #2
## COMPARISON: MARCH TO THE BEAT OF YOUR OWN DRUM

*"Comparison is the thief of joy."* —Theodore Roosevelt

No two purposes are identical. As a result, it is impossible to compete against anyone other than yourself when it comes to living on purpose. I repeat, it is *impossible* to compete against anyone other than yourself. The sooner you accept this, the sooner you can stop wasting your time agonizing over other people's pursuits and how they're doing exactly what you want to do, but faster, better, or for less money than you are.

Remember, you are the only person on earth at this moment and time with the set of experiences, talents, and character traits it will require to live out *your* purpose. If you are committed to listening to your inner voice and following its guidance—one action step at a time—no one will be able to replicate your exact journey. You will be operating in a league of your own. You will be marching to the beat of the only drum that really matters: yours.

When you pursue someone else's purpose or "borrow" a purpose from one of the many success stories the media indoctrinates us with on a daily basis, you're no longer in a league of your own. You've unwillingly signed yourself up for a race you simply cannot win. You cannot win because you were never meant to. You were not designed to compete in that race.

This is where a lot of us get stuck. We set out to achieve a goal without asking ourselves whether it's a goal that matters to us in the first place. Instead, we pick a goal that matters to our parents, partner, boss, colleague, or the most popular kid in school. If you don't do the work to get crystal clear on your *why*, you will find yourself adopting other people's. This is a recipe for disaster because when you inevitably keep failing to achieve someone else's goal, you will grow increasingly frustrated. This can go on for decades. After a while, the experience of feeling like a failure will start to impact other areas of your life. You will slowly start to lose your confidence and desire to do anything—let alone try something new or different— moving you further and further away from living in alignment with your purpose. The more you fall short, the more likely you are to default to a safe, prepaved path that will only exacerbate this vicious cycle. (If it works for them . . .) In reality, the best thing you can do in this situation is take yourself out of the unwinnable race and chart your own path. Comparing yourself, your purpose, and your progress to someone else is a pointless, lose-lose endeavor. You will end up resenting yourself and those you compare yourself to, which may include close friends or former idols.

If I had allowed myself to fall into the comparison trap, this book would have never been written. For starters, it feels like everyone and their mother is writing a book these days. Even though I know that's not *actually* true (only a very small percentage of people become published authors), it certainly felt that way when I was deep in the trenches. It's like the infamous red car syndrome: as soon as you purchase a red car, all you see are red cars. Everywhere. When I was about 80 percent done with the first draft of my manuscript, Oprah published her book *The Path Made Clear*. It was a short, but powerful, summary of what several of her guests on the *SuperSoul Conversations* podcast had learned on their path to purpose. I stopped writing for a good two weeks. "What's the point?" I thought. Oprah is the *queen* of personal development—what could I possibly have to say that will hold a candle to her guests, including the likes of Deepak Chopra and Jane Fonda? Then I reread what I had written so far and realized that I was missing the point. (Ironically, mind you, the point I was trying to make.) The point is that I am *never* going to be better at this than Oprah or Deepak. But I don't have to be. I just have to follow my truth—my why— and trust that it will be enough to touch someone, somewhere. If Oprah had compared herself to other talk show hosts back when she was starting out, it might have deterred her from blazing the trail that she did. How much less rich would our world be without the wisdom she has bestowed on us over the years?

## *PURPOSE PLAYS:*
### TACTICS TO AVOID THE COMPARISON TRAP

1. **Catch yourself in the act.** The next time you find yourself slipping into a comparison trap, acknowledge it and take action. Express what you're feeling out loud to a friend or a loved one, so they can help you identify what's driving your desire to compare. Then, do some-

thing to shift your state (ideally, related to one of your Purpose Triggers): go on a walk, listen to your favorite song, curl up with a good book, or volunteer at a local nonprofit—whatever floats your boat!

2. **Don't borrow the why, borrow the how**. Only once you are clear on your why can you start to look to others for inspiration. Instead of copying their *why*, borrow their *how*. Because when it comes to how you are going to live out your purpose, "success leaves clues," as Tony Robbins says. Find people who have succeeded at what you want to do and ask yourself (or ask them directly): What are they doing differently? What steps did they take to achieve their goal? What advice would they give themselves if they were to do it all over again? Robbins calls this approach "modeling": finding role models, studying their trajectories, and applying their learnings to your own path.

   Modeling is not comparison. It's not about you versus them or better versus worse. It's about capturing data points and applying proven strategies that will help you become even more effective at pursuing your own one-of-a-kind journey.

3. **Remember that all purpose *is* created equal.** Everyone is designed to serve a different mission. If we were *all* meant to be social workers or missionaries, the world would be a terribly boring and dysfunctional

place. We *need* people who are called to develop creative solutions to complex business problems just as much as we need people who are called to heal or advocate on behalf of those who cannot. One purpose is no more worthy or valid than another, so stop judging yourself (and others) for having a purpose that doesn't have an obvious "save the world" connotation. Similarly, don't put yourself on a pedestal if your purpose happens to more visibly benefit others. We are all here to pursue what lights us up, and that thing is different for everyone—for a reason. Merging onto someone else's highlighted route because you think it might be better received is a surefire way to be miserable.

## *PURPOSE BLOCKER #3*
### GUILT: ANGER TURNED INWARD

*"Guilt is anger turned inwards."* —Denise Morrison, former CEO of Campbell Soup Company

I first heard this quote around a dinner table with fourteen young female leaders in the food industry and Denise Morrison, the CEO of Campbell Soup Company at the time. The dinner was part of a program we were running for the company in an effort to help their executive team gain a better understanding of the behaviors and preferences of a new demographic.

While the discussion may have *started* with food, we didn't linger on that topic for long. As you can imagine when a group of ambitious twenty- and thirty-something women have the opportunity to learn from a successful Fortune 500 CEO, they all have one question on their mind: how to pursue their professional goals without sacrificing their own well-being or their ability to show up for their friends and families. In other words, how does one juggle these competing demands and still manage to stay sane? Without fail, Denise would start by debunking the myth that "work-life balance" was anything more than a false pretense: sometimes you have to miss an important meeting to make it to your daughter's ballet recital, and sometimes you have to miss a bedtime ritual to wine and dine a prospective client. One day you have to disappoint a friend in order to set a boundary, and the next day you have to miss your favorite yoga class in order to spend quality time with your partner. Life happens—and there's nothing balanced about it. By striving for a perfect balance, we are setting ourselves up for failure. Instead of accepting this and practicing compassion, however, most of us resent ourselves for falling short. We get frustrated when we can't be in two places at once or please *everyone* at the same time. This frustration turns into anger and, ultimately, guilt.

The original definition of guilt implies that an actual crime has been committed or that a violation of some sort has taken place: someone is "guilty" of something. Yet 99 percent of the time, humans feel guilty about situations that do not warrant so much as an eye roll, let alone the amount of self-torture we put ourselves through. We can even feel guilty about doing the *right* thing sometimes, simply because it may disappoint someone (perhaps someone we don't even like). Most guilt is entirely self-imposed and entirely unnecessary. Women are notorious for falling into to this particular trap. We set unreasonable expectations and are unreasonably hard on ourselves when we can't live up to them. As Madeleine Albright says, "guilt is every woman's middle name."

If we can get ourselves into this mess, however, we also have the power to get ourselves out of it. The most effective antidote to guilt is forgiveness. Forgive yourself by letting go of the judgment you place on your decisions and your actions. Forgive yourself so you can stop agonizing over something that's in the past. Forgive yourself for being unable to meet someone else's needs because you took responsibility for your own. Accept that you did the best you could and *move on*.

Finding and pursuing your purpose may require you to shift your priorities, albeit temporarily. If you're a notorious people-pleaser who tends to put yourself last on your to-do list, this process may feel a tad self-indulgent. You may think it's "selfish" to take time away from your work, your chores, or your family, and it can set the all-too-familiar cycle in motion. Let's fast-forward to a future version of you. Imagine you finish this book with a list of action items you want to take in order to incorporate more of your Purpose Triggers into your daily life. You're excited. But as soon as you put the book down, a little voice inside your head starts whispering to you: Who do you think you are? Do you really think you can transform your life overnight and ignore all the people who are counting on you to stay the same? You become frustrated with yourself, angry even, because you *know* you deserve this. You have put your needs behind others' more times than you can count. Instead of expressing the emotional saga taking place between your ears, however, you keep it to yourself and make up any number of guilt-inspired stories to validate the voice: "My parents didn't pay for my degree in physics so that I can pursue dance full-time." "I should be spending my free time volunteering like my friend does, instead of writing my book." "My child will never forgive me if I miss this soccer game to pitch a prospective client." Sound familiar? It's time to break this pattern once and for all.

## *PURPOSE PLAYS:*
## TACTICS TO FEND OFF GUILT

So how do you foster enough forgiveness to stop guilt in its tracks? It comes back to the number one rule of survival: put your own oxygen mask on first before helping others. No one expects (or needs) you to be a martyr. What your family, your friends, and the rest of humanity *need* is the best possible version of you. The version that's living in alignment with your purpose and contributing your unique gifts to the world in a way that fills you up beyond belief. Indulging in this journey guilt-free will make you a better friend, colleague, parent, child, and overall person, so do us all a favor and give yourself permission to invest in *you*.

I want you to take a moment to recommit to your Purpose Statement. Pull it out of the drawer or flip back to the appropriate page in this book and read it out loud several times. Now, make a list of all of the ways that living in alignment with these words will enable you to show up more fully for your loved ones. Then reflect on the list and ask yourself: Is the juice worth the squeeze? I am willing to bet the answer is a big fat *hell yes*.

# PURPOSE BLOCKER #4

## IMPOSTER SYNDROME: DO UNTO YOURSELF

*"No one can make you feel inferior without your consent."* —Eleanor Roosevelt

When it comes to your purpose, it really only takes one to tango. It takes *one* person to make or break your dreams. That person, my dear reader, is you. It's a lot of responsibility, I know. But if you don't believe in yourself, how can you expect anyone else to believe in you? At the end of the day, *you* are the only person you can control. (Trust me, I've tried). So you have to be your biggest cheerleader. No ifs or buts about it.

In our live workshops, I've seen countless people commit to the exercises, fighting tears as they remember the activities they adored as a child and recognize how little time they are carving out for these passions today. They craft the most beautiful Purpose Statements and can pinpoint the exact moment(s) when they feel most alive. Fast forward to when it's time to take action, however, and they're stumped. The daydreaming is easy—it's the doing that's hard. Yet the only difference between dreaming about something and making it happen is believing that you are worthy—that you deserve to have that thing. I am continuously surprised at the number of people for whom this is an insurmountable block. They know what their purpose is and they even know exactly what steps to take to design their life around it, but before they can make any progress toward their goals, they fabricate a laundry list of excuses as to why they aren't worthy of pursuing it: "I'm not good enough,"

"I don't have the right credentials," "who cares what I have to say," and so on and so forth. It's so common that researchers created a term to describe it—imposter syndrome: the fear of being exposed as a fraud.

If this sounds familiar, I beg you to stop. You are probably one of the first people to cheer on a friend who is doing something bold in pursuit of their dream. You might show up at her fundraisers, shout encouraging words from the sidelines as he competes in his first race, and purchase far too many unnecessary products from her Etsy store. Why? Because you believe in them. And because you know that your encouragement means the world to them.

So why not give yourself that same grace? Why not cut yourself some slack? I'll say it again because it's worth repeating: if you're not willing to bet on yourself, why should anyone else take a chance on you? Here's what I know for sure: believing in yourself doesn't guarantee success, but *not* believing in yourself *does* guarantee failure. So instead of listing all the reasons you *can't* do something, redirect this energy toward finding one reason you *can*. What do you have to lose?

## *PURPOSE PLAYS:*
### TACTICS TO CHEER YOURSELF ON

1. **Repeat after me.** I am not a big mantra girl, but this is one instance where it can come in handy. Stand up straight, plant both feet firmly on the ground, and repeat after me (yes, out loud): I am exactly where I'm

supposed to be. I am here for a reason. I am in control of my destiny. I am enough.

Pick one or all of these phrases and recite them out loud at least five times a day, every day, until you start to *believe* in the words (and in yourself).

2. **Be your own cheerleader.** If you've ever competed in a sports event or performed on some type of stage, you may recall looking up at the crowds or into the audience and seeing your friends or family waving a sign with your name on it: "Go, Ben, Go!" "You can do it, Claire!" When you're performing at your best, these words might draw a smile. But when you're struggling to tread water, this small sign of support can mean the difference between throwing in the towel and making it to the final buzzer. When someone shows up for you or invests in you, you want to show up for that person in return. You want to prove to them that you're worthy of their support. Here's the thing, though: people are busy and distracted. They may not have time to create a sign for you. In fact, they may not even be aware that you need one in the first place. Stop waiting for someone else to cheer you on. Write a handful of motivational slogans or quotes on sticky notes and put them on your mirror, your desk, and the dashboard of your car. It sounds cheesy, but it works. Most days, you won't even notice them; but on the days when your purpose

feels like a distant memory, these notes will help you keep your head in the game.

3.  **Squash negative self-talk.** We are much harder on ourselves than on others. For most of us, this behavior is so automatic that we've become immune to the digs we dole out all day every day. When I look in the mirror after rolling out of bed, my first thought is usually "ouch, look at those bags." It's not only mean—it's also terribly unproductive. So I challenged myself for thirty days to say this instead: "Hello, beautiful! What are we going to do to make today count?" I know this sounds cheesy. I'll be honest, the first few times, my immediate reaction was: "Well, we're going to start with some makeup because that face sure isn't leaving the house." Over time, however, it's become a new (and considerably healthier) habit that has had a profound impact on my mood. When is the last time you complimented someone else? (Within the last week, I hope.) Now when is the last time you gave *yourself* a compliment? Exactly. So next time you feel your inner bully bubbling up, don't throw yourself a pity party—give yourself the same grace and empathy that you would offer a friend.

4.  **Treat yourself.** I mean this in every sense of the word. Self-love is having a moment right now. Every blogger, influencer, and brand seems to be promoting it—often alongside images of bubble baths and indulgent snacks.

While these visuals may appear frivolous on the surface, the underlying message behind the social trend is a worthy one. Given how easy it is to criticize one another these days, it is more important than ever to have your own back, and to give yourself the love and attention you deserve. There are many ways to practice self-love. For some, it's hitting the snooze button. For others, it's planning a solo vacation. Another great way to honor yourself is to see a therapist. If you're struggling with a lack of self-esteem and find that it's preventing you from living your life to the fullest, for example, this might be the kindest thing you can do for yourself.

# PURPOSE BLOCKER #5
## EXPECTATIONS: SET YOUR OWN BAR

The land of expectations is where purpose goes to die. How many times have you stopped yourself from doing or saying something because you were afraid other people *expected* something else from you? Or because you anticipated a certain response from them? Notice that both of these instances imply *perceived* expectations. More often than not, you have no idea what the other person is *actually* thinking—but this doesn't stop you from making up a story around it and letting that story determine your course of action. Take my friend Tim. He was convinced that his parents would disapprove of a career change he was hoping to make, so he stayed in a job that made him miserable for almost five years. They had been so proud when he got the job offer; after they had invested most of their savings in his education, accepting the offer was the least he could do, Tim thought. Five years later, when it got so bad that he was even willing to live with the consequence of disappointing his parents, he quit. It still took him several weeks to find the courage to tell them. When he finally did, they were almost more relieved than Tim was. "All we ever wanted is for you to be happy," they said. "We've known for years that this job was sucking the life out of you."

"So why didn't you say something?" Tim asked incredulously.

"Because that isn't our job anymore. It's your life, honey."

Tim will never forget the lesson he learned that day. It was a lesson in self-respect. Tim learned that the only person he had to answer to was himself. He had willingly given up ownership over his own life—he had willingly played the victim card—because of a made-up story. He had wasted several years of his life by buying into a false expectation instead of trusting himself to know best.

When someone calls you smart, you are *expected* to do well in school. When someone calls you athletic, you are *expected* to make the team. When someone calls you skinny, you are *expected* to stay that way . . . aren't you? For the longest time, I resented others for putting this type of pressure on me. As soon as I was given a label like this, however flattering, I instantly felt pressure to live up to the associated expectations. It was exhausting, not to mention stressful. When I didn't get an A on a test, a wave of anxiety would wash over me—I felt like I was disappointing everybody who had once referred to me as intelligent.

It took a long time for me to realize that no one else truly cared if I got an A or a B+. The only expectations I had to overcome were my own. Sure, my parents would *prefer* me to get the better grade, but in the grand scheme of things, how I did in school was a lot less important to them than who I was as a person. In an episode of the podcast *Hurry Slowly*, Jocelyn K. Glei explores the simple but profound question: "Who are you without the doing?" That question hit home for me. I have dedicated so much of my life to *doing*— most of it in an effort to live up to expectations, either my own or those I perceive others have for me. Who would I be if I stopped working so damn hard on this? How would I know if I was valued? How would I know when I'm on the right track? How would I make my parents proud or my husband happy?

Then I was reminded of something my dad used to say. He has a lexicon of "Dadisms," some of which are cringe-worthy, but this one is pure parenting gold. As a child, I never paused to consider how profound it was—in fact, I barely gave it a second thought. But after listening to this podcast episode, it dawned on me how lucky I was to have heard these words on a regular basis: "Thank you for being you." To this day, he still signs off his text messages with it sometimes. It may not sound like much, but what my dad was trying to tell us is that he loves us *without the doing*. He loves us even when we don't win our games, get straight As, or live up to his (or anyone else's) expectations. I only wish I had internalized this sooner, as I could have saved myself years of unnecessary anxiety.

I am not recommending that you give up on expectations altogether. They can be a good thing, in some cases. If you suffer from low self-esteem, for example, you may only start to see your true potential through the expectations that others have for you—it suggests they believe you were meant for more. That being said, it's important to give yourself permission to ignore them sometimes, especially if they are deterring you from acting on the little voice inside your head. Don't let a perceived opinion or fabricated story stop you from living out your dreams. Don't be like Tim. You can continue to point fingers and play the blame game all day long, but you will eventually realize that there is only one person at fault—and that's you.

## *PURPOSE PLAYS:*
### TACTICS TO OVERCOME EXPECTATIONS

1.  **Set healthier expectations**. Just because you've started jogging doesn't mean you have to run a marathon next month. Be mindful of what your own expectations are and ask yourself if they are helping or hurting your cause. In some instances, setting the bar high can be incredibly motivating. In others—like my jogging example—it may stop you from completing the first 5K or loop around the block. Why bother if you're not going to be the best, right? Wrong. There is so much more to learn from being a beginner. If you always expect yourself to excel (or imagine others expect you to), you will constantly find yourself falling short—or let the fear of falling short prevent you from ever starting in the first place. If you notice that you're trying to live up to an unrealistic expectation, or comparing your beginning to someone else's end, give yourself permission to set a new one. This doesn't mean you shouldn't

challenge yourself—it means that you should be smart about *when* to do so.

2. **Take responsibility for your own expectations.** A lot of the expectations we attribute to others are actually our own expectations in disguise. Refrain from blaming or resenting other people and take responsibility for the pressure you're putting on yourself. If other people expect something from you that you can't or don't want to deliver on, it's up to you to speak up. Be honest with them about how you feel and what you want, so they can set more realistic expectations for you too.

3. **Take a personality test.** Self-awareness is paramount in this context. A personality test can highlight areas in which you may be particularly sensitive to other people's (perceived) opinions. It can also indicate how you might respond to these expectations—will you be excited to rise to the occasion, or will you be inclined to run and hide? Knowing how you're wired can help you become more attuned to this potential Purpose Blocker and anticipate how it might hold you back. A few of my favorites include the Meyers-Briggs Type Indicator, DiSC Personality Profile, Human Design, and the Enneagram Test.

4. **Surround yourself with people who love you without the doing.** Be thoughtful about who you spend your time with and how they might be influencing what you do, and most importantly, what you *don't* do. Not everyone is able to verbally express how much they care about you, like my dad does, but surround yourself with people whom you feel comfortable with when stripped of all your accolades, accomplishments, and aspirations.

# *PURPOSE BLOCKER #6*

## FEAR: THE MOTHER OF ALL BLOCKERS

*"Feel the fear and do it anyway."* —Susan Jeffers

Most Purpose Blockers come down to the same inescapable source: fear. Fear of failure, fear of what others might think or say, fear of making the "wrong" choice, fear of losing something or someone. The list of potential things to fear is never-ending, and it can be quite paralyzing. But the sad, hard truth is that nothing in life is guaranteed. You can lose everything in an instant without doing anything to "deserve" it. The rumors are true: life isn't (always) fair. Bad things can (and do) happen to good people.

I don't say this to scare you. I say this to set you free. Because if you can't control the outcome, why waste your time stressing over all the possible scenarios that might ensue? When you live in fear, you're living in *one* potential variation of the future—a variation that is highly unlikely to materialize, mind you. Your time is much better spent focusing on what you *can* control: your attitude. Are you going to let your fear consume you, or are you going to let it fuel you? If you succumb to the former, it will be very difficult to embrace your true purpose. You will always be making concessions in an attempt to avoid whatever you fear—in an attempt to stay small. In other words, fear is living your life *for* you. But if you learn to dance with your fear—to coexist and perhaps even *co-create* with it—you will no longer be beholden to its power. You can redirect this anxious energy towards something more productive. You can fearlessly embrace the life you're meant to live.

Susan Jeffers, the psychologist and self-help author who became famous for the words at the outset of this chapter, is an excellent example of someone who danced with fear. She was married at the ripe young age of eighteen and had two children shortly thereafter. Her husband had a high-profile job, and Susan soon realized that she was expected to stay at home with the kids. She felt trapped, not to mention bored out of her mind. But instead of accepting her fate, Susan packed her bags and moved the family to New York, where she went back to school to get a degree and a doctorate in psychology. This might not sound fear-inducing today, but keep in mind that she did this in the 1960s, when women could not have a credit card or serve on a jury in most states. Then, after sixteen years of marriage, Susan left her husband—an act that was far less acceptable back then than it is now. A divorce (and the societal judgment that often accompanies it) can easily provoke a negative spiral of emotions, but Susan later described it as "the most empowering event of her life." Her attitude was challenged once again when she was diagnosed with breast cancer. She recovered and eventually credited her illness for connecting her to her second husband. Susan's story highlights that life is what you make of it: you can choose to give fear power over you, or you can choose to overpower your fear. If Susan had let fear get the best of her, she would not have gone on to write eighteen books, appear on *The Oprah Winfrey Show* thirteen times, and build a network of licensed Feel the Fear trainers who continue to share her teachings across the world. She would not have lived on purpose.

I love learning about stories like Susan's because they are a welcome reminder that fear is universal. Even the most successful, purpose-oriented humans experience "oh shit moments" every once in a while. If you've ever read an autobiography or listened to a long-form interview with just about any celebrity or world leader, you will hear about the countless obstacles they've had to overcome. These people aren't just "lucky"—even though they're often the first to admit where luck did play a part in their rise to fame. What truly sets them apart is that they persevered *in spite* of fear. They had so much trust in themselves and their purpose that they were able to find a way to "keep calm and carry on" no matter how scary each step was.

## PRODUCTIVE VERSUS UNPRODUCTIVE FEAR

The first step to dancing with fear is learning how to identify what type of fear you're dealing with. There are two types of fear: productive fear and unproductive fear. Productive fear is healthy—it protects us. Centuries ago, when we were hunters and gatherers, fear could mean the difference between life and death. Fear alerts us to potential danger and ignites a fight-or-flight response that is essential to our survival. If you're swimming in the ocean and spot a big white fin in the distance, you will instinctively start swimming in the opposite direction or scream at the top of your lungs. That's productive fear.

In the absence of wild animals and enemy tribes, however, the modern mind has a hard time distinguishing real danger (e.g., a hungry great white shark) from something that is simply unknown or uncomfortable. You may feel scared shitless before walking into your boss's office to give your two weeks' notice or before you hit "publish" on a very personal blog post, but the likelihood that either of these situations will turn out to be life-threatening is quite slim. Your body may still respond as if it's in grave danger, however: your heart will start to race, your stomach will be doing somersaults, and your mind will make up a million excuses as to why it is a horrible idea. That's *unproductive fear*.

It's unproductive because it's deterring you from the situations that actually hold the greatest potential for personal development. As Neale Donald Walsch famously says: "Life begins at the end of your comfort zone." From this point of view, fear is the enemy of growth. It may save your ass every once in a while, but most of the time it's doing everything in its power to keep you in a safe bubble of familiarity. Left to its own devices, fear can easily drown out your inner voice and wedge itself in between you and your purpose like an unwelcome third wheel.

So the next time you feel afraid, overwhelmed, or anxious, ask yourself: is this productive or unproductive fear? Is there a chance I could get seriously, physically hurt (or hurt someone else) by doing this? If the answer is no, you are most likely dealing with *un-productive* fear. This is the type of fear that can make an excellent salsa partner.

## *PURPOSE PLAYS:*
### TACTICS TO DANCE WITH FEAR

I've boiled it down to a five-step process:

1.   **Call it out.** The worst thing you can do is ignore the fear. Instead, you want to feel it fully. Accept that whatever resistance you're feeling is grounded in unproductive fear and remind yourself that it's *only human* and that you are not alone. Often, it helps to share your fear with someone else as it instantly reduces the power it has over you. Fear is a fact of life, and it doesn't discriminate based on race, age, socioeconomic status, or national-ity. When expressed, fear has the potential to unite us by building connection around a shared experience. Unfortunately, we are more inclined to do the opposite. We ignore the fear and internalize it, where it quickly translates into shame, anxiety, or any other number of negative emotions that can block your path to purpose. So express it already! (You may even find that you're do-ing someone else a great service by sharing.)

2.   **Play it out to the end.** Make a list of the worst pos-sible thing(s) that could happen if you went for it and

failed. Take the time to climb up anxiety mountain and sit on top with each of these scenarios. How would you handle them if they did occur? Confronting your fears and making them specific will reduce your anxiety about them. Often you will find that they seem less scary or less likely than you had thought. Then, make a list of the best possible thing(s) that could happen if you succeeded. What would your life look like? How would you feel? Compare the two lists.

3. **Ask yourself "what if?"** Ask yourself what you would do if you didn't have that fear. What would you do if your fear of failure, public scrutiny, lack of resources, or whatever it might be, did not exist? What opportunities would open up for you? What would you do differently?

4. **Remind yourself that fear is an illusion.** It's just a story your mind is telling itself to keep you operating inside of your comfort zone, even though all the good stuff is waiting just outside this imaginary bubble of safety.

5. **Fuck the fear and do it anyway**. Take a bold step toward your goal. It doesn't need to be a big leap—even a small step is enough to generate the forward momentum you need to overcome anxiety mountain. See how

that feels, give yourself a pat on the back, and then do it again. And again.

I know how scary this is. You believe that as long as you don't *fully* put yourself out there—as long as you stay within the confines of your comfort zone—you can't *fully* fail or fall flat on your face. Or so you think. What I've learned is that while you may think you're protecting yourself, you're actually just cheating yourself (and everyone else, for that matter) because you're keeping the best parts of who you are hidden. These parts will only shine if and when you trust in them enough to take a risk and be vulnerable in the name of purpose.

# CHAPTER TEN

# PURPOSE ENABLERS

Now that we've covered some of the obstacles you might encounter on your purpose journey, I'd like to introduce you to the essential tools every purpose-seeker needs in their toolkit. If you were a contestant on *Who Wants to Be a Millionaire?*, Purpose Enablers would be your lifelines. They are meant to help you course-correct when you inevitably encounter a Purpose Blocker and guide you back to the highlighted route. More importantly, however, if you learn how to use these tools correctly, they can significantly decrease the likelihood that you take a wrong turn in the first place. You may find yourself gravitating toward different Enablers at different points of your journey. Pick and choose whichever tools work for you based on your needs in the moment—whether you're looking for clarity, community, or a firm kick in the behind.

## PURPOSE ENABLER #1

### JOURNALING: REFLECT, RELEASE, RECOMMIT

*"I can shake off everything as I write; my sorrows disappear, my courage is reborn."* —Anne Frank

Journaling is one of those things you either do or wish you did. I fluctuate between both extremes depending on the state of my psyche at the time. Despite my inconsistency, however, I have experienced the power of journaling firsthand and believe it to be especially valuable on the path to purpose.

For some reason, my journaling has historically spiked around new romances. In elementary school, I used to dedicate an entry to each of my crushes; in high school, I would fill page after page with pained he-loves-me-he-loves-me-not fodder that seems terribly dark and dramatic in hindsight; and finally, in college, I described in detail how my now-husband and I first met and fell in love. Since that turned out to be my last *new* romance, what followed was a ten-year hiatus. I would occasionally write a few paragraphs about something I didn't want to forget, but it was sporadic at best.

I didn't get back into a consistent writing practice until my yoga teacher training a few years ago. We were required to buy a journal on the very first day of class and were given daily journaling assignments. The self-awareness we would cultivate by reflecting on our experiences on and off the mat would allow us to incorporate these insights into our teaching. It felt terribly awkward to me at first. I would write what I thought my coach wanted to read, even though I knew he wouldn't *actually* read it. But the more I forced myself to write, the easier it became. Soon, I was journaling about far more than my aspirations as a yoga teacher or how my practice felt that day. It became a way to process and make sense of whatever thoughts were swirling around in my monkey brain. While I will admit that I haven't been nearly as consistent since then, I am far more inclined to pull out my journal whenever I feel stuck, frustrated, or particularly grateful for something.

If you're the type of person who needs hard evidence before giving something a try, there are plenty of studies on the positive outcomes of journaling. Some of the most unexpected benefits of journaling are a stronger immune system, better sleep, more self-confidence, and a higher IQ.[9] Not to mention the myriad of ways it has been shown to reduce stress, depression, and other mental illnesses. Journaling is a healthy habit to start no matter where you are in life, but it can be particularly helpful on this journey. As you may have learned during your Discovery Missions, there's a lot of "stuff" hiding in our subconscious. Journaling is a way to get that stuff on paper so you can reflect on it, process it, and move on. Journaling is also a great way to address Purpose Blockers. It's like a free therapy session with your wisest, most clairvoyant self.

## JOURNALING TO TURN UP THE VOLUME

Journaling is one of the easiest ways to connect with your inner voice. It starts like any therapy session would—with a brain dump of whatever is on your mind. Once you clear those cobwebs, you can start to ask your inner voice questions and respond to them directly on the page. It can take a little while to develop a rapport with your inner voice, but be patient. You might be surprised by what comes up when you let go of judgment and distractions and create a safe enough space to confront what's really going on, behind the stories.

It turns out that your inner voice is an exceptional therapist.

First of all, she doesn't charge. Second, you never have to worry about her breaking the client confidentiality clause. Finally, she's an excellent listener and will only interject when she knows you're not being honest with yourself—as long as you're willing to genuinely listen to her. A journaling practice can hold you accountable. It's an opportunity for you to ask yourself the tough questions and for you to answer them truthfully. It can also help you strengthen your self-awareness, which is essential to living on purpose.

I'll give you an example of a typical journal entry. I usually start by describing something concrete that happened that day. Let's say I had dinner with a girlfriend—I'll call her Lucy. I will say all the things I would want others to believe about my dinner with Lucy first: *I'm so grateful for this friendship. Lucy seems to be very excited about this new opportunity at work, and she totally should be; I would be too, but it's not really for me because I've never wanted to have that much responsibility.* That's when my inner voice will jump in: "Is it really not for you? Are you really unable to handle that amount of responsibility?" I may try to find another excuse, but eventually I will admit that I *am* a little jealous and that I *do* in fact want what Lucy has. That part of me resents her for unapologetically going for it, while I can't—or won't—even admit that I want it. "Why *can't* you have that thing?" my inner-voice therapist will ask empathetically. Before I know it, I am filling page after page with insights on whatever limiting belief or story is holding me back. Twenty minutes of journaling later and I feel like a new woman. Not only am I better able to support Lucy, but I may even ask her for advice on how I can follow in her footsteps.

## JOURNALING TO PROCESS

Journaling is often prescribed to people who have experienced trauma or are battling PTSD. This makes a lot of sense, as the most effective way to process an emotion or a complicated feeling is to express it, and journaling enables you to do exactly that. By describing the emotion or feeling, you are able to label it and thus distance yourself from it.

I am reminded of this every time I read my own past journal entries. What seemed overwhelming and all-consuming at the time now sounds completely trivial and, frankly, like a waste of paper. Our mind really can (and does) play tricks on us: it can blow something out of proportion, giving it far too much power or weight. Fortunately, putting something into words allows you to evaluate a situation or emotion from a more objective, rational point of view.

One of the best parts of journaling is that it forces your mind to slow down. You can only write so fast, even in chicken scratch. Studies have shown that journaling allows you to process what you're writing in real time. There's often no need to reread what you wrote because the act alone is enough to release whatever resistance you were experiencing. The things we feel compelled to journal about often hold important clues to our purpose or the blocks and stories that may be holding us back. So the next time you feel a strong emotion—whether it's a positive emotion like gratitude or love, or a negative emotion like jealousy or anger—grab your journal. You may not know exactly what you'll learn when you put pen to paper, but I highly encourage you to *just start writing*. Consider revisiting the ground rules I shared in Chapter Four, as these may come in handy:

1. Do not self-edit.
2. Set a timer.
3. Use pen and paper.
4. Do not embellish.
5. Set the mood.

## JOURNALING TO SET GOALS

Last but not least, journaling can be a great tool for turning intention into action. Living in alignment with your purpose takes discipline—especially when you're just getting started—and it can be helpful to set concrete goals for yourself. The act of writing down these goals increases the likelihood that you will attain them. By articulating each objective and putting it in writing, your commitment is intensified and you're more likely to hold yourself accountable.

Once you've written down your goal(s), there are a few additional journaling exercises I recommend. Imagine your goal is to find a new job, for example.

1. **Write down three action steps that you're committing to take in the next thirty days in order to make progress towards your goal.** Each action step has to be simple, specific, and measurable. In other words, there's no gray area—you either completed the action step or you didn't. Using our example, your action steps might be to: 1) update your resume by next Friday, 2) reach out to three people who have jobs you might be

interested in and ask them to coffee, and 3) apply to at
least three jobs by the end of the month.

2. **Anticipate what type of resistance you might experience and journal it out.** Write about the Purpose
Blockers that may come up and describe how you
plan to overcome them. Refer back to the previous
chapter for specific strategies you might want to employ. In this example, you may expect to encounter
imposter syndrome: what if I'm not good enough for
this job? Journal about where you think this thought
is coming from and the mantras you will use to build
your confidence.

3. **Finally, journal about what it will feel like to reach
your goal.** Describe a day in your life as if you have already achieved it. Back to our example of finding a new
job, you would describe what time you wake up, how
you feel on your way to work, how you feel when you
get home, the impact that you're having in your new
role, how it will impact your relationships, and so on.

# JOURNALING TIPS FOR NON-JOURNALERS

Journaling did not come naturally to me. I fought hard to make it a habit, and it still requires a healthy dose of self-discipline to turn to my journal instead of my social feed.

Here are some tips for those who can relate to my struggle:

- Pick a page at the front or back of your journal and write down your Purpose Triggers and your Purpose Statement. This way, you can refer back to them frequently and remind yourself *why* you're on this journey to begin with.

- Consider having multiple journals—one in your bag or on your desk and one on your bedside table. That way you are always ready to write when the mood strikes.

- Keep a note on your phone so you can write down quick insights or prompts you want to journal on when you have more time.

- Start with what you're grateful for. There is *always* something to be grateful for (the sunshine, your health, a warm bed, a perfect cup of coffee . . .) so it can be a good way to get started when you're struggling to find a topic to write about.

- Make it part of your routine. Find a time each day or week that works for you and try to be consistent about it. Sundays are a great day to journal because you can reflect on the past week and set goals for the week ahead.

- Consider a "One Line a Day Journal" or a journaling app, which are designed with non-journalers in mind.

- Let go of any pressure you feel to fill the page. Sometimes you have a lot to say, and sometimes a single sentence or word does the trick. Just be consistent about writing.

- Set the mood. Meditate or listen to your favorite tunes before you start to journal. A little effort can go a long way.

# PURPOSE ENABLER #2

## CREATE A PURPOSE PACK: FIND YOUR PEOPLE

*"Find a group of people who challenge and inspire you, spend a lot of time with them, and it will change your life forever."* —Amy Poehler

I love Amy Poehler. Not just because she's hilarious, but because she's *real*. There are a lot of celebrities I would be excited to meet, but there are very few I think I'd actually *like*. Amy is one of them. She feels like the warm, self-deprecating older sister without whom family holidays would be significantly less entertaining. But she is also the sister you can go to for some sage advice on the messy, hard things in life. What confirms this hunch for me is the tight-knit group of powerhouse women who never seem to leave Amy's side, including Tina Fey and Maya Rudolph. That's a rare type of friendship for us muggles in the "real" world, let alone in Hollywood. There aren't many people in the spotlight who genuinely seem to enjoy each other's company as much as these ladies do. They're in each other's movies, they celebrate each other's birthdays together, and they're the first to promote one another's passion projects (no matter how terrible they are). Amy has found her Purpose Pack, and we can all learn a thing or two from how she invests in these relationships.

## WHAT IS A PURPOSE PACK?

The word "tribe" has become quite a buzzword in recent years. I am sensitive to the cultural connotations of the term and believe some uses of it have been justly criticized, but I am more interested in what its trending status says about society today. Yes, its popularity may be partially driven by the fact that it rhymes with "vibe" and looks great on a printed T-shirt, but I think its prominence is fueled by a growing desire for human connection in our digitally driven world.

Finding and cultivating your Purpose Pack may not be *essential* to living on purpose, but it will make it a whole lot easier (and more enjoyable). Having a squad to support you on this journey can serve several important objectives. For starters, they can cheer you on during times when your own energy or self-confidence is running low. They can also act as a helpful sounding board and call you out on your BS, which is especially helpful when identifying and overcoming your limiting beliefs. Finally, they can inspire you by leading by example—by pursuing their own purposes on their own terms. You are a product of your environment, so one of the best things you can do to set yourself up for success on this journey is to surround yourself with a wolf pack of fellow purpose-seekers.

When I refer to your Purpose Pack, I'm not just talking about the people you spend the most time with. In fact, your Purpose Pack may include people you haven't seen in ages. It's not about the quantity of time you spend with them; rather, it's the *quality* of the relationship that counts. We all have people in our lives who we can go years without seeing, only to pick up right where we left off. They're the people who don't care if you miss a birthday or an important milestone because, you know, life happens. They're the people who are far more interested in how *you* are doing versus your bank account or your career. They're the people who have your back and are genuinely invested in your long-term success—however you choose to define it. These are "your people." (And if you *don't* have these people in your life, it's time to find them! They're out there, I promise.)

## DEFINE YOUR PACK

It won't come as a surprise that the most important ingredient for a pack-worthy relationship is *trust*. I don't just mean trust in the conventional sense of the word. Of course, you will want them to be trustworthy, but you also have to be able to trust that your pack will hold you accountable to living up to your potential, even when it means pushing you beyond your comfort zone. You have to trust that they will always act in your best interest, even if you may not see it that way *yet*. You have to trust that they will tell you the truth, even when it's the last thing you want to hear.

Beyond a foundation of trust, there are several other common traits that characterize a pack-worthy relationship:

1. **Your pack looks past what *is* and sees what *can be.***
   They don't just see the person you are today, but the person you *can become* if (and when) you step into your true potential. They are the people in your life who believe in you unconditionally and will not let you settle for anything less than what you deserve (and are capable of). They are the friends who push you to think bigger. They see the horizon, even when you lose sight

of the highlighted route, and they will gladly jump in the passenger seat to help you navigate.

2.  **Your pack allows you to be 100 percent yourself.** In fact, they demand it. Your pack is made up of the people you feel most comfortable around. It's a judgment-free zone. They are the friends you call to celebrate the highs *and* commiserate the lows, no masks or makeup required. Your pack members aren't afraid to call you out on your own BS. You may actually find that you avoid these people in the moments when you are not being honest with yourself, out of fear that they will see right through the act.

3.  **Your pack expands your view of what's possible.** I am borrowing this term from Lacy Phillips's manifestation formula. An "expander," according to Lacy, quite literally expands what you believe is possible for yourself by modeling it. They give you an example to grow into or toward. The individuals in your pack do not have to be expanders in all aspects of your life, but they should ideally model at least one behavior or character trait you are working toward yourself. As you embark on this journey, it's important to surround yourself with people who are living (or aspiring to live) in close alignment with their own purpose. Remember that this will look different for everyone. For some, it may look like an influential business leader; for

others, it may look like a full-time super mama or the ultimate family man who somehow manages to prioritize health and friendships amidst a crazy demanding schedule. Take note of what you admire most in each of your pack members; observe and learn from them so you can incorporate these best practices into your own life.

4. **A pack-worthy relationship is *always* mutual.** There's a reason you seek each other out. Whether you care to admit it or not, these individuals consider you to be an expander for them as well. Even if they seem light-years ahead of you in some ways—based on empty metrics like years of experience or the size of their personal network—I guarantee you they have something to learn from you too. Like Ralph Waldo Emerson said, "Every man is my superior in some way." Besides, things may *look* perfect on the outside, but you're rarely seeing the whole picture. A pack-worthy relationship is one of equals, so avoid putting these people on a pedestal. You may not realize it, but you could be creating unnecessary (and unwelcome) pressure to live up to *your* ideal, ultimately detracting from their ability to offer expansion from an honest, authentic place.

## HOW TO RECOGNIZE YOUR PEOPLE

There is no magic number when it comes to your Purpose Pack, nor is there a perfect profile of a pack member. They can be family members, old friends, new friends, mentors, neighbors, colleagues, even pets in some cases. I am also not suggesting that you exclusively hang out with your Purpose Pack from here on out. Your social network can be as inclusive as you want it to be. What I *am* saying, however, is that it's important to identify the individuals who will not let you play small—either by encouraging you to play big or by modeling what it looks like to play big—and be intentional about spending time with them.

Start by creating a list of the people who may already be part of your unofficial wolf pack today. Ask yourself the following questions:

> Who do I call first when I have something to celebrate?
> Who do I call first when I'm sad or down?
> Who do I call when I need a pep talk?
> Who knows me better than I know myself?
> Who brings out the best in me?
> Who makes me feel seen and heard?
> Who inspires me to take action?

There's a good chance that the same two or three names come up in several of your responses. That's an indication these individuals are part of your pack (or should be). If no one came up, don't sweat it. Start by identifying celebrities or public figures who represent your *ideal* pack members based on their personalities or the content they share—for example, my girl Amy Poehler. Social media and podcasts can be a great place to find these expanders. Then, once you get a better sense of the types of qualities that resonate with you, proactively look for people in your immediate vicinity (assuming you don't run in celebrity circles) who embody these same traits and ask them out on a friend date.

Don't feel like your pack members all have to be friends with each other. They may never even meet—although it's a special treat when they do. You may also find that you have several different subpacks for different interest areas. As mentioned, your pack members don't have to be expanders in *every* dimension of your life. You may have a professional pack who you turn to for career-oriented advice and mentorship; one or two couples that represent #relationshipgoals; a friend who has health and wellness routines down to a tee; and a few individuals who make you want to be a better friend yourself because they always show up exactly when you need them to and know exactly what to say. In general, you can probably talk to any of your pack members about *any* topic and get an enormous amount of value from the conversation, but there is often one particular area that they are each world class at.

## *PURPOSE PLAYS:*
## TACTICS TO BUILD YOUR PURPOSE PACK

Once you've identified your pack members, invite them on this journey with you. If they don't feature prominently in your life today, make a concerted effort to see or hear more of them. Whether you're reconnecting with an old friend or diving deeper with someone new, here are some tips on how to cultivate pack-worthy relationships:

1. **Be vulnerable.** The best way to deepen a relationship is to put yourself out there by sharing something real, raw, and scary. It creates an immediate connection because the other person feels honored that you are willing to trust them with something so personal. It instantly breaks the ice and sets the tone for the relationship. More often than not, it's reciprocated.

2. **Don't be afraid to go first.** Building on the previous point, sometimes you have to be brave enough to be the *first* person to share. Yes, it can be terrifying, and yes, you may get burned if someone doesn't respond in kind, but it's worth the risk if the person has potential pack status.

3. **Give as much as you get (and then some).** Show up for your pack. This is a two-way street, and the more you give, the more you will receive in return. Always add value where you can, whether it's sharing connections, expertise, or advice, or simply *listening* when they need an ear.

4. **Create a safe space.** For your Purpose Pack to do its "job," you have to be open to receiving honest feedback from them. My husband is part of my pack, and the first

time I read him a passage of this book he promptly list-ed several areas for improvement. Tears sprang to my eyes, and I immediately got defensive. Being the good husband that he is, he apologized and started retract-ing his earlier comments in an effort to calm me down. The next day, once the emotions had subsided, I recon-sidered his comments and realized he was right. In fact, he made some excellent points that would make the book *that* much more compelling. I made the edits, thanked him for his candor, and continued to share my work with him. I don't always agree with his feedback, or incorporate it for that matter, but I have learned to trust that his critique is *always* driven by his desire for me to thrive as a person and as a writer.

## PURPOSE ENABLER #3
### SELF-DISCIPLINE: GIVE YOURSELF AN EDGE

*"Discipline is the bridge between goals and accom-plishment."* —Jim Rohn

I am willing to bet quite a lot of money that if you allowed me to observe your morning routine, I could predict—more often than not—whether you will succeed on this journey. (Meaning, whether you will go on to live in greater alignment with your purpose af-ter reading this book.) What does my morning routine have to do with it, you might be wondering? Well, everything. Because how you start your day is a reflection of how self-disciplined you are. Do you wake up when your alarm goes off? Do you brush your teeth—even if you're in a rush? Do you choose the donut or the omelet for breakfast? While these might appear to be trivial decisions, they can have dramatic consequences for the way you live your life. The more self-discipline you possess, for one, the less each of these instances will feel like a decision. When the moment arrives, there's only one option in your mind: You wake up. You brush your teeth. You eat the eggs.

One of the biggest differences between those who take action toward their purpose and those who don't is self-discipline. So, if you want to live on purpose, one of the best things you can do is develop this muscle. Yes, willpower is best described as a muscle, rather than a talent or character trait. The positive implication is that you can *train* yourself to be disciplined. People aren't born with either a strong or a weak willpower muscle—it's an equal playing field for all. On the flip side, however, muscles can get fatigued over time, and willpower is no different. You may be able to say no to that donut at 8:00 a.m., but if it's still there when you get home after a long day at the office and a fight with your partner, the likelihood that you can resist it a second time is a lot lower.

Discipline can sound like a harsh word, because it's often associated with punishment—parents discipline their children; people discipline their dogs; teachers discipline their students. But self-discipline is a little different. Most of my self-discipline was cultivated through extracurricular activities. Perhaps you can relate—whether you played soccer, violin, or chess, it required consistent, (ideally) daily practice. It was presented to you as if there were no choice in the matter. I remember getting home from school every day and begrudgingly sitting myself down at the piano to complete my fifteen minutes of scales. While I complained about it then, I sometimes miss the dogmatism. It felt inevitable, and therefore, it always got done.

I still remember how disoriented I was after my family dropped me off in my New York City apartment—a walk-up on 37th Street. It was the first time I was left entirely to my own devices. I could do whatever I wanted. There were no professors who were expecting me to show up for class or hand in my homework. There was no coach who was counting on me to make it to practice on time. And there was no parent to make sure I didn't eat pizza three days in a row. I had complete control over what I did and when I did it. Instead of feeling a marvelous rush of freedom like I had expected, I felt like I was about to have an anxiety attack. I remember thinking, what's the point of doing anything if no one cares anyway? It took me a few months to realize that there *was* someone who cared—immensely—about my decisions: my future self.

At the heart of self-discipline is a deep respect for oneself. When you're self-disciplined, you can count on yourself to honor the commitments you make. You know that when you plan to work out the next morning, you will wake up when your alarm goes off; you know that when you commit to finishing a project, you will get it done. This might sound like nothing major, but it's a BFD. Think about how much energy and anxiety you're wasting on self-doubt. Think about how much more time you will have to dedicate to the things that matter when you know that the basics—like brushing your teeth and eating your vegetables—are taken care of. Everyone has a flaky friend—you know, that person who consistently bails last minute or arrives forty-five minutes late. Don't be that friend to your future self.

Besides, self-discipline can give you an enormous leg up on your quest for purpose because it creates a solid foundation on which to build. In yoga, we refer to discipline as "tapas." It's one of the five "niyamas," which are best described as moral codes that yogis are encouraged to follow in order to grow both on and off of the yoga mat. *Tapas* is derived from the Sanskrit word "tap," which means "to burn." It is often translated as "inner fire"—it's what drives you to wake up before the sun rises, to show up day after day to practice, and to breathe through challenging poses instead of giving up on them. It's what establishes those critical building blocks you can come to rely on. Without this inner fire—without a strong foundation—you would never feel free enough to experiment in class, to explore a new pose, or to balance all your weight on one limb. This relationship between grounding and freedom is just as present outside the yoga studio. Living in alignment with your purpose requires a foundation of self-discipline because only when you can trust that you are fully supported will you feel truly free to pursue your curiosities, take chances, and be vulnerable.

## *PURPOSE PLAYS:*
## TACTICS TO DEVELOP SELF-DISCIPLINE

1. **WWYFST: What Would Your Future Self Think?**
   Get acquainted with your future self. You might even

want to give him or her a name. Whenever you feel tempted to give in to an unhealthy urge that will lead you astray from your highlighted route, check in with future you. What decision or choice would they want you to make? What can you do today to set *them* up to thrive tomorrow?

2. **Establish rules for yourself.** Your parents aren't the only ones who can impose a curfew. Identify what your nonnegotiables are—the daily habits or decisions you want to commit to in order to live in greater alignment with your purpose—and set some ground rules. For example, if one of your Purpose Triggers is exercise and you're trying to make it part of your weekly routine, create a rule that you work out on Mondays, Wednesdays, and Fridays. *That's just what you do,* no excuses. So when you wake up on Monday morning, you put on your sneakers and head to the gym. It's no longer a choice; it's who you are.

3. **Start small.** The beauty of self-discipline is that it begets more self-discipline. It's like a domino effect. If you're able to cultivate it in one area of your life, it will eventually bleed into another. So don't worry about tackling your biggest, toughest weakness from day one. If you know you're a sucker for sweets, start by developing discipline at work or as part of your morning routine. Commit to waking up at the same time every

day or to clearing your inbox before you head home at night. I guarantee that after a few weeks of committing to these changes, limiting your sweets intake will feel a lot more manageable.

4. **Reward and forgive yourself generously.** Reward yourself for sticking to the rules—it's important to celebrate the wins, after all—but remember that we are all works in progress. Developing self-discipline, especially if it's a muscle you haven't flexed before, requires a lot of energy at first. Try to strike the balance that every parent aspires to: don't come down so hard on yourself that you won't be able to get back on the horse, but be disappointed enough that you won't want to repeat the transgression again.

5. **Remove obstacles by having a plan.** We all have a kryptonite. Mine includes chocolate and cooking shows. Once I start snacking or press play on *The Great British Baking Show*, it's not just a slippery slope—it's an all-out avalanche. I cannot stop before I've polished off the entire bar or finished the full season. These may not appear to have a direct connection to my purpose, but once you lose control in one area of your life, it doesn't take long before you start breaking other rules. No amount of self-discipline can eliminate every urge, but you can limit these setbacks significantly by having a plan in place. In my case, I only buy bars

that are 85 percent cacao—unlike caramel-filled milk chocolate, one square of this dense chocolate is often enough—and I limit my cooking shows to weekends only. Identify your kryptonite and come up with a strategy for minimizing the likelihood that it throws you off course completely.

## PURPOSE ENABLER #4
### MOMENTUM: RIDE THE WAVE

*"A body in motion stays in motion."* —Isaac Newton

Do you ever imagine what your life would be like if it were a movie? More importantly, if it had a soundtrack? I do. I'll be walking down the street and know exactly what song would be playing in the background. Experiencing true momentum is like hearing Freddie Mercury belt the chorus of "Don't Stop Me Now" on repeat. It's that feeling of flow, when things effortlessly fall into place—one small win leads to the next, and you're "on a roll," as they say. Momentum can be a powerful tool when pursuing your purpose. Especially if you're the type of person who tends to fall prey to procrastination, momentum may be the secret weapon you've been waiting for.

I used to play field hockey in college, and one of my coach's favorite things to yell from the sidelines was, "Read the momentum of the game!" It took me an entire season to figure out what she meant by this. According to her, a team that has just scored a goal is always more likely to score again. Not because they are the better team per se, but because they have momentum. If the opposing team scored on us, our only objective was to double down on defense and do everything in our power to break their momentum and stop them from getting another point on the board. If we scored, on the other hand, we would move into an aggressive full-court press to ride the momentum wave. I have no idea if my coach's theory is backed by actual data, but in theory, it makes sense. Immediately after a goal is scored, the team's confidence is at an all-time high, and this is often reflected in their play: they start to anticipate one another's next move, they take the right risks at the right time, and they come together in what appears to be a perfectly choreographed dance—often leading to another goal.

Even if you've never played field hockey (or any sport, for that matter), this phenomenon may sound familiar. Have you ever had a day where you felt unstoppable? You move and shake everywhere you go, crossing things off your to-do list like it's no big deal. The more you get done, the more accomplished you feel, and the more things start to fall into place. That's momentum.

The best part about momentum is that it can be generated by anyone, at any time. All you need is that first small win. Moreover, the longer you're able to sustain momentum, the less effort is required. It's like pushing a boulder up a hill. The hardest part is getting the boulder to move in the first place. Most of your energy is dedicated to that first inch of progress. You may have to throw yourself up against the boulder, grit your teeth, and tense every muscle in your body to get it into motion. But, as the boulder starts to roll, less and less force is needed—until eventually one steady hand does the trick.

The challenging part about momentum, however, is that it's fragile. It's highly sensitive to outside forces. Imagine for a moment that your path to purpose is that boulder. It can be brought to a standstill by any number of things, several of which were addressed in the previous chapter on Purpose Blockers. Your boulder may be rolling along merrily one moment, only to be stopped in its tracks by a seemingly "harmless" comment from someone in your environment the next. That person will have no idea how much work they may have just negated, but once your boulder stalls, you're back to square one. You will have to generate an enormous amount of strength and willpower to set it back in motion.

## *PURPOSE PLAYS:*
### TACTICS TO GENERATE MOMENTUM

In addition to eliminating Purpose Blockers, the best way to (re) create and maintain momentum is to take small, consistent steps toward your goal. Simply put, momentum is generated when you continue to put one foot in front of the other for extended periods of time. So how do you know what actions to take in order to keep your boulder in motion? This is where your Purpose Triggers come in.

The next time you're in need of that first small win, come back to your triggers. Create a list of straightforward, minimal-effort actions you can take to align yourself with your Purpose Triggers. Ideally, these actions can be completed within an hour and should not be dependent on a third party.

For example, if your Purpose Trigger is related to music, your list of actions might include:

> Create a purpose playlist on Spotify
> Have a mid-day dance party for one
> Go to a local open mic night
> Grab your instrument of choice and play for fifteen minutes
> Belt out your favorite song in the shower

Or, if your Purpose Trigger is related to being outdoors, your list might be:

> Go on a walk
> Have lunch outside
> Plan a weekend hike with friends
> Open your windows while you work

These small commitments can have an outsized impact on your state of mind. Tony Robbins often refers to the power of "changing your state." He achieves this through more radical measures like jumping on a trampoline or standing in a negative 200-degree Fahrenheit cryotherapy chamber, but even the smallest change in our environment can spark a chain reaction. Opening a window one day might lead you to eating lunch outside the next, and perhaps walking the day after that. Each action will release the feel-good endorphins that accompany accomplishment and set you up to take another positive step towards your purpose. Momentum is all about focusing on the next best step—not the pie-in-the-sky goal—until your boulder is cruisin'.

## *PURPOSE ENABLER #5*
### DECLUTTERING: CREATE SPACE FOR WHAT MATTERS

*"Clutter is the enemy of clarity."* —Julia Cameron

This is not about getting rid of stuff. It's about eliminating unnecessary clutter from your life and your space, so you can create more room for what matters most. It's about being intentional when it comes to the people and the possessions you choose to surround yourself with. It's about controlling your space, instead of letting it control you.

As you can imagine, finding and pursuing your purpose is considerably easier when you're operating from a spacious, clear state of mind. However, the reality is that most of us are battling an endless barrage of thoughts, fears, and anxieties at any given time. Buddhists call this phenomenon the "monkey brain" because it's like a monkey swinging from branch to branch—thought to thought—without ever pausing to soak up the present moment. Unsurprisingly, they recommend meditation as a way to temporarily tame the monkey and quiet the mind. Meditation is an invaluable tool, and I highly recommend it as part of your purpose toolkit, but I am also acutely aware that it takes time to cultivate a consistent meditation practice. Moreover, a lot of people never fully warm up to the magic of meditation. So here's an alternative approach to achieving inner zen: create outer zen *first*. You may not be able to control the mess in your mind, but you can *always* control the mess in your environment.

## DECLUTTER YOUR WORK SPACE

Whether your office consists of a desk, a kitchen table, or an art studio is beside the point. Whatever space you choose to "work" in should be held sacred. (Note that I am referring to "work" in the broadest sense of the word here. Whether you're being paid to perform a task or doing the deep inner work required as part of this process, your environment should set you up for success.) It should inspire you to show up as your best self and be free of any distractions so you can remain laser-focused on the objective at hand: sharing your gifts with the world. Chefs refer to this as "mise en place," which freely translated means "everything in its place." If you don't know any chefs personally, you may be surprised to learn that they are notoriously meticulous. As a result, high-end commercial kitchens are some of the most well-organized work environments you'll come across. If you've ever worked in one, you'll know that the first two things the kitchen staff are required to do upon arrival are clean and chop. Every ingredient is washed, cut, and prepped to perfection. What's more—with the exception of certain staples—only the items featured on the menu that night are allowed in the kitchen. Arriving in the kitchen, the chef is met by neat containers filled with presliced and marinated food items. This enables the chef to focus all her attention on what she does best: cook a mouthwatering meal for the customer. She is not distracted by a messy counter or missing ingredient. Can you imagine how much less anxious you would be if your own mise en place was that on point?

Understandably, some (work) environments are more flexible than others, so you will have to operate within your limitations. Regardless of the setting, however, these six steps can help you design a space that reflects the outer calm you wish to achieve on the inside:

**Step 1.**   Place all the objects in your (work) environment in one big pile on the floor.

**Step 2.**   For each object, ask yourself:
a) Does this serve a purpose?
b) Does this serve a purpose for me *right now*?

**Step 3.**   Discard all the items that do not serve a purpose, and store all the items that don't serve a purpose for you *right now* in a box or a closet.

**Step 4.**   Ask yourself if anything is missing. Are there any objects that would improve your ability to do your best work, such as a specific type of pen, a picture of your loved ones, or a favorite quote? Add these items—but make sure they serve a distinct purpose.

**Step 5.** As you redecorate your space, be intentional about your mise en place. Ask yourself "why" you think an item belongs in a particular spot—you'll be surprised at how often the answer is "because it's always been there" or "because that's where most people keep it." Challenge these preconceived notions.

**Step 6.** Make sure whatever *does* get a coveted spot is ready to be used. If one of your Purpose Triggers is hiking, prepare a backpack with all your hiking supplies: a water bottle, energy bars, sunscreen, etc. so you can head out the door whenever the mood strikes! If one of your Purpose Triggers is writing, unpack your new notebook and make sure there's a pen next to it.

I recommend revisiting this process every six months to avoid any unconscious hoarding.

## DECLUTTER YOUR CALENDAR

There is no question that time is our most precious resource—and yet it's the one we tend to undervalue the most. Perhaps because it's particularly hard to measure the value of time compared to other, more tangible, assets. Consequently, it's very challenging to calculate a "return" on your investment of time. This is how I found myself in the busyness trap. I had started equating busyness with productivity. The busier my calendar, the more productive—and thus valuable—I felt. It never occurred to me that not all activities were equally worthy of my time. What's worse, some activities actually made me *less* productive because of how draining they were. Sound familiar?

Because this journey will require you to make time for new activities that better align with your Purpose Triggers, it's imperative that you learn to protect your time and be deliberate about how you choose to spend it. Start to view every hour on your calendar as a valuable piece of real estate and embrace the fact that not every hour of every day needs to be filled. The more open space you can create, the better—because space is exactly what your purpose seed needs to grow into a mature source of fulfillment.

If you can't reduce the number of activities on your calendar, try consolidating them. One of the best decisions my cofounder and I ever made for our business (and our sanity) was to implement no-meeting Mondays and Wednesdays. It's exactly like it sounds—at all costs, we avoid scheduling any calls or meetings on Mondays and Wednesdays. Yes, the other days of the week are often booked solid, but knowing that we have at least two whole days to work undisturbed allows us to stay present during each and every interaction. Before we implemented this policy, we often found ourselves multitasking on calls, which typically backfired as we would have to spend twice as much time catching up on what we missed. Since making the change, however, we now enjoy much more space to think creatively. It also enables us to be more strategic about how we choose to spend this time. Whereas in the past we were constantly reacting to incoming requests and putting out fires, we're now able to take a step back, reflect on our to-do list, prioritize what matters most, and develop a plan of attack. By consolidating and clearing our calendar, we took back control of our time.

## *A PURPOSEFUL USE OF YOUR TIME*

An excellent way to use the space you create in your calendar productively and purposefully is for activities related to your Purpose Triggers. If movement or exercise is one of your Purpose Triggers, for example, block off an hour each day (or every other day) to do something that gets your blood flowing. Some days, it may be a quick walk around the block, or a ten-minute ab set in your office, while other days you may go to an actual exercise class. If writing is one of your Purpose Triggers, block off twenty minutes before the rest of your house wakes up, or during your lunch hour, to journal.

It goes without saying, but when penciling in time for Purpose Triggers, avoid obsessing about them. Yes, you want to prioritize the things that light you up. And yes, taking action requires discipline and consistency. But remember that this is also meant to be sustainable. When they feel too forced, these activities can quickly become draining, which is exactly the *opposite* effect of what this exercise is meant to achieve.

## DECLUTTER YOUR MIND

Once your external environment has achieved a state of zen, it will become infinitely easier to mirror this on the inside. But there's one more tool I want to share—and that's the power of living in the present moment. We spend a surprisingly small amount of time here. You might be wondering if I'm going crazy because how can you live anywhere *but* the present? I'm not referring to your physical body, however—I'm referring to your mind. How much of your day do you spend either living in the past (characterized by guilt or regret) or living in the future (characterized by anxiety and fear)? More than you probably care to admit. But think about it—if we were fully immersed and focused on the present moment, there would be nothing to worry about. Yet we spend an enormous amount of time pondering woulda-shoulda-coulda scenarios.

When you're operating in the here and now, it becomes much easier to see things clearly because you aren't experiencing the emotions that arise from living in the past or the future. A clear mind is an invaluable asset on your path to purpose because it allows you to make decisions from an unbiased, unobstructed point of view. So, in addition to decluttering your external world, I recommend taking some time to identify the activities that bring you a greater sense of clarity and calm. (These may or may not overlap with your Purpose Triggers.) Examples could include:

Meditation
Exercise
Reading
Listening to music
Listening to a podcast
Focusing on your breath

Whatever your preferred method might be, ritualize it. Make it part of your daily or weekly routine and prioritize it. When you find yourself in a monkey state of mind, stop whatever you're doing and turn to this activity.

Ultimately, this is an exercise in intentionality. *Physically*, being thoughtful about the environment you create and the activities or people you allow in. *Mentally*, being thoughtful about what you choose to focus your attention on. By creating space, you create opportunity. More importantly, you are putting yourself in a position to take advantage of that opportunity because you won't be distracted or drained when it presents itself.

## WHAT IS YOUR ONE WORD?

Every year, my husband and I do our New Year's resolutions together. There are quite a few steps to our annual ritual, but my favorite part is choosing our word. This one word represents our personal "theme" or focus for the next twelve months. In the past, some of my words have been *play*, *optimize*, and *invest*. In 2019, my word was *space*. I chose it for a number of reasons, including my desire to write this book. I knew that it was going to be a massive project (to say the least) and that it would be very easy to come up with a million excuses as to why I couldn't or shouldn't follow through. But I also knew that it was what I *had* to do to live in alignment with my purpose. So I made a conscious decision to create enough space for myself to get it done. I wasn't exactly sure how or what it would look like, but as soon as I had articulated *space* as my word for the year, I started to embody it. I felt less anxious about blocking off weekday mornings to write and more at peace when I had to cancel Saturday plans with friends to do some more research for a chapter. My word became my anchor and my permission slip—a guiding light reminding me of my purpose and how I had chosen to pursue my why that year.

Even if it's not January first, I encourage you to come up with your own word for the year ahead: What word best encapsulates the energy you want to embody in order to make progress towards your goals?

When you have your word, make sure you refer back to it often. I write mine in my journal and on a sticky note that stays on my desk. Every time I see one of these reminders, I instantly ask myself where I am successfully creating space and where I still have room to improve.

# PURPOSE ENABLER #6

## REFRAMING: ADOPT A FRESH PERSPECTIVE

*"A successful man is one who can lay a firm foundation with the bricks others have thrown at him."* —David Brinkley

When working with our corporate clients, we often draw on a creative problem-solving technique called "design thinking." The term was first coined by David Kelley, a professor at Stanford University and the founder of the world-renowned design consultancy IDEO. In essence, design thinking is about creating products and services from a user-first point of view. It starts by developing empathy with the end user or consumer, so the designer has an intimate understanding of their motivations, behaviors, and preferences. Once you understand the specific pain point(s) you are designing for, the next step is to brainstorm as many solutions to the problem as possible. This stage is all about quantity over quality and often involves copious amounts of sticky notes. From there, you start to filter the various solutions based on feasibility and other constraints you may need to consider, such as budget or time frame. When you have narrowed it down to a handful of viable solutions, you run a series of pilots with the end user to capture their feedback and identify the potential pitfalls of your idea. Ultimately, the goal is to deliver a product or service that has a much greater likelihood of adding value and being adopted by your audience, compared to something that was designed in a lab based on a set of assumptions.

One of the most frequently used tools in design thinking is "reframing." At its core, design thinking encourages you to reframe people's challenges as innovation opportunities. But reframing is embedded in each step of the process. Imagine that you work at a place like IDEO and have been hired by a large grocery store chain to solve the following problem: seniors are struggling to reach the products on the bottom shelves. Your first step is to reframe this challenge as an opportunity: "How might we enable seniors to more easily access products on the bottom shelves?" According to the design thinking process, you would then take it one step further and reframe the question at least three times to make sure you're asking the *right* question to begin with. For example:

How might we enable *individuals with lower mobility* to easily access any product they want, no matter where it's placed in the store?

How might we enable individuals with lower mobility to *purchase* any product they want, no matter where it's placed in the store?

> How might we enable individuals—no matter their
> mobility level—to easily purchase what they want
> *without ever having to enter the store?*

Do you see how solving for this last question will not only benefit seniors, pregnant women, and people with back problems, but *all* customers—even those who aren't able to get to the store? Moreover, it focuses on the *actual* desired outcome, namely the purchase, versus the ability to access a product and put it in your cart. This highlights how reframing the objective can result in a dramatically different question and, more importantly, outcome.

Without realizing it, you are constantly experiencing life through different frames. These frames act as filters, influencing the way you interpret or process information and imagery. Just about anything can be "framed" in a positive or negative light, depending on your personal interest in the matter, the stories in your head, and even your mood at any given time. It's all in the eye of the beholder, as they say. Some days, my cofounder can give me a critical piece of feedback and I will graciously acknowledge it and thank her for her honesty. Other days, that same piece of feedback elicits a passive-aggressive response and quickly tailspins into an argument.

Learning how to take a step back and apply different frames to a specific situation is an incredibly powerful skill. It will not only make you a more empathetic person, but a more creative one too. When we're in the thick of things, we tend to think there is only *one* way to approach something or *one* correct answer, but this is an incredibly limiting lens to look through. A simple reframe can open up a world of new potential solutions, which is particularly helpful if you find yourself facing a roadblock on your highlighted route. The next time you find yourself in this situation, instead of giving in to frustration, stagnation, or even despair, view it as an opportunity to experiment with different frames. Run your situation through a few of the reframing exercises included here, and you'll be dreaming up innovative solutions in no time.

## REFRAMING WITH ROLE PLAY

One quick way to reframe a situation is to look at it through someone else's eyes. Next time you hit a roadblock, ask yourself:

- How might I approach this problem if I had a million dollars?
- How might I approach this problem if I had zero dollars?
- How might I approach this problem if I were James Bond?
- How might I approach this problem if I were Wonder Woman?
- How might I approach this problem if I could learn any new skill overnight?
- How might I approach this problem if I only had twenty-four hours to find a solution?

It will require some old-fashioned imagination, and you may come up with ninety-nine horrible ideas, but the hundredth idea might be exactly what you need to keep moving forward.

## PURPOSE PLAYS:
## TACTICS TO REFRAME YOUR REALITY

1. **"I have to." >>> "I get to."** We all like to be in control of our own destiny as well as our daily decisions. As soon as you feel like you have to do something, it feels like a burden. It feels forced—and none of us enjoy that feeling. Yet we use this terminology—"I have to"—all day, every day, even in situations where there is absolutely zero pressure or urgency involved. By saying that you have to do something, you automatically diminish your ability to derive joy from the activity in question because it feels like it's cramping your style: "I have to go to this dinner tonight." "I have to work on my book all day." "I have to take the kids to the park." Try reframing these sentences by using "I get to" instead: "I get to go to this dinner tonight." "I get to work on my book all day." "I get to take the kids to the park." Don't you feel much better about your plans already? It not only feels less burdensome, but it also evokes gratitude because it suggests that you have an opportunity to take advantage of rather than an obligation to fulfill.

2. **"I can't." >>> "I won't."** Setting boundaries is a critical skill when you're refocusing your attention on the people and projects that matter most to you. You only have so much time and energy to give, after all. I don't

know about you, but whenever I have to say "no" to something or someone, I find it very hard to justify unless my reasoning includes an "I can't": "I can't come tonight because I have another engagement." "I can't run the race because I hurt my ankle." "I can't quit my job because I need the money." This not only leads me to say yes to too many things that don't actually fill my purpose cup, but it also insinuates that I'm the passenger rather than the driver of my own life. Start to pay attention to your choice of words and how often you use the phrase "I can't" when establishing a boundary. Try reframing it to "I won't" instead and see how it feels. Personally, I find it to be much more empowering, which has the positive side benefit of muting feelings of guilt or regret.

3. **An excuse >>> a reason.** I have learned a lot from watching my friends become mothers. Every one of them is a rock star in my eyes—even though they all approach this new chapter in their own perfectly imperfect way. One friend in particular comes to mind. She has two kids under the age of two and still manages to get her twenty-five-minute workout in five days a week. "How do you do it?" I once asked her in awe. "It's not always easy," she admitted, "but I view my girls as my reason to stay in shape, not as an excuse not to." This made so much sense to me. Not only will she be better able to keep up with her ac-

tive little ones when she's chasing them around the yard, but she is also showing them the importance of prioritizing self-care. If you find yourself making excuses as to why you're putting off your purpose, try reframing it as a reason to pursue your purpose instead.

4. **Victim >>> victor.** I have alluded to the dangers of the victim mentality several times in this book. Mostly because it's a very common blocker, but also because a lot of people don't even realize that they're stuck in victimhood. They've become so accustomed to the frame that life is happening to them that they're unable to consider that life might be happening for them instead. You always have a choice: are you going to rise to the occasion and be the hero of your own story, or are you going to let the circumstances get the best of you? A victor mentality not only gives you greater confidence in your ability to overcome just about any obstacle, but it also opens your mind to a whole new world of creative solutions. When you view yourself as a victor instead of a victim, it's never a question of whether you'll be able to come out victorious, it's just a matter of how. So, when you're feeling stuck or uninspired, answer honestly: are you in victim or in victor mode?

5. **Failure >>> feedback.** This is perhaps the most clas-
   sic reframe of all. John Danner, a former professor
   of mine, wrote a book on the topic of failure called
   *The Other "F" Word.* The book uses a variety of corporate case studies to indicate that failure shouldn't
   be feared as the opposite of success, but rather embraced as a critical part of any "successful" endeavor.
   Danner and his coauthor even created the "Failure
   Value Cycle," which describes all the ways a company can benefit from failure as they move through
   each step of the process. When it comes to finding
   your purpose, I believe there is an analogous "Failure Value Cycle." At each step along the way, there is
   an enormous amount of learning to be gleaned from
   failing—but only if you acknowledge the failure and
   choose to reframe it as an opportunity for growth. Every time you recognize that you failed to listen to your
   inner voice, for example, you are fine-tuning your
   inner compass and are thus less likely to make the
   same mistake again. If you refuse to acknowledge a
   miscommunication when it occurs, however, you will
   miss out on this potential evolution. Accept that failure is going to be part of the process—whether you
   like it or not; so, instead of working so hard to avoid
   or ignore it, make the conscious decision to embrace
   failure when it happens and milk it for all it's worth.

Now that we've covered the most common blockers you might face and the enablers you have access to, I want to take a closer look at how to cultivate more purpose in four of the most important dimensions of our lives. Specifically, I am going to look at work, relationships, play, and money. I selected these four dimensions because they are the most universally relatable and significant when it comes to living on purpose—irrespective of age, culture, career status, religious beliefs, or country of origin. While you might struggle with one particular dimension over another, the chapters that follow are meant to offer insightful observations, case studies, and exercises for every reader—no matter how aligned or misaligned you might be today. I will explore how to infuse each dimension with a greater sense of purpose by drawing on your Purpose Triggers and the tools I have shared so far. Finally, you will design your own roadmap to purpose in chapter 15 with the Purpose Plan, which is organized around these same four life dimensions.

# CHAPTER ELEVEN

# *WORK*

" *Build a life, not a resume.* "
—Jay Shetty

We spend a significant percentage of our waking hours working. Consequently, a lack of purpose at work is often the most palpable for many of us. You would think, then, that it would be harder to ignore a lack of engagement in this area of our lives, but this isn't always the case. Many of us consider our work to be an extension who we are—part of our identity. Personally, I've discovered that it's also a big part of my feeling of self-worth. After rebuilding my professional reputation from scratch seven years ago, my ego has become quite attached to our Fortune 500 client list. It offers a false sense of confidence and credibility, making it all the more challenging to consider a potential career shift toward writing and coaching. The thought alone stirs up all the insecurities I experienced the last time I took an untraditional turn. I'm terrified of "undoing" all the hard work and losing my identity as a "successful" professional woman. It took quite a bit of time and journaling to arrive at this aha moment, because it implies that, despite knowing better, I am *still* prioritizing someone else's definition of success over my own. I am afraid that others will see me as less intelligent, less productive, or less impressive as a writer. There, I said it. We are all works in progress. This is one of *my* stories—and I'm working hard to reframe it—but it's just one example of the many narratives that might be preventing you from pursuing your purpose if it requires a significant transition in your professional life.

For those of us who consider our career to be part of our identity, admitting that we're not fulfilled at work is no easy feat. In fact, we would generally prefer to keep our head in the sand because as soon as we acknowledge it, there's no going back. Returning to my shoe analogy, the hardest part is that the discomfort isn't always unbearable. This makes us more prone to conveniently ignore or endure the feeling. On top of that, many of us don't actually believe that we have access to (or deserve) something better—so, naturally, we settle. It would almost be easier if there were a more visceral sense of dread or dissatisfaction because it might force us to take action sooner. But the reality is often more measured. You hit snooze one too many times in the morning, you start the countdown to Friday on Monday afternoon, and find yourself shying away from stretch opportunities that feel like "too much work." You are definitely not fulfilled by your work, but it's *bearable*.

If this sounds familiar, it's time for a kick in the *pantalones*. (And I say this in the most affectionate way, given that I have been in your shoes several times in my relatively short career.) This is a gross waste of human potential. If there's one thing I want you to take away from this chapter, let it be this: you are fully capable of finding work that is aligned with your purpose. Moreover, if you already know what that work is, you are fully capable of overcoming any stories or obstacles that are standing in your way.

If you've started making a mental list of reasons that I'm wrong and that you *can't* make the move (you're not good enough, you won't be able to make a living, it's irresponsible, people will lose respect for you, and the list goes on!), I suggest you take a step back and ask yourself why this truth is so hard for you to accept. Perhaps you have some limiting beliefs around purpose and work to unpack? For example, if you grew up in a household where one or both parents were constantly complaining about their job or struggling to find and keep a job, it's very likely that you unconsciously inherited this unhealthy point of view. You may not even have noticed how your past is subconsciously sabotaging your future.

Fortunately, I'm here to tell you that there's an alternative: you have the opportunity to not only *love* what you do but to find an exorbitant amount of meaning and purpose in your work. The best part is that it has precious little to do with your job title—or your salary, for that matter. Studies have shown that a janitor can find just as much purpose in their work as a neurosurgeon who saves lives for a living (and makes millions doing so). So what *does* it have to do with, you might be wondering? It comes down to two things. First and foremost, self-awareness—clarity around what it will take for you to thrive in your professional life. In other words, a clear understanding of what matters most and thus what you need to optimize your work around. Second, mindset—because, as you've learned throughout this book, attitude is *everything*.

While we're on the topic of self-awareness, you might want to consider whether finding purpose in your work is even a priority for you. Because while I maintain that you are fully capable of finding a job that's aligned with your sweet spot, not everyone wants— or needs—to derive their sense of purpose from a nine to five gig.

## KNOW YOUR TYPE

At the most macro level, there are two types of people. One is in no way better or worse than the other, but it's important to understand what camp you fall into. The first type of person *must* derive their sense of purpose from what they do. I say "must" because they truly believe they have no choice. Spending hours a day on something that simply pays the bills but is not aligned with any of their Purpose Triggers feels soul-crushing to these individuals. Take my friend Andrew, for example. He earned a degree in finance and got a prominent job at a great accounting firm straight out of college. Four years later, he quit his job to become a full-time artist, supporting himself by waiting tables on the side. He makes a fraction of what he used to make as a consultant, but he's never been happier. While it might appear to some as if Andrew is taking the easy way out and blindly following his passion with no regard for the consequences, nothing is further from the truth. It can be incredibly challenging to belong to this group. It often requires major sacrifices—financial, social, romantic, geographic—because the alternative would mean showing up as a shadow of your true self. It would mean shutting down the part of you that makes you *you*—the part of you that is born to create, heal, write, teach, or whatever it is that lights you up.

The second type of person does not feel the need to rely on a job to fulfill their purpose. They *work to live*, focusing on all the ways they can pursue their purpose *as a result* of the income they earn or the lifestyle they are able to create. No one wants to be *miserable* at work (and no one should settle for that dismal scenario), but these individuals are perfectly happy finding fulfillment *outside* work through hobbies, travel, relationships, you name it. If you fall into this camp, the key to thriving is being intentional about incorporating your Purpose Triggers into your leisure time.

If you instantly related to one of these two types, that's great. There is incredible power in knowing and owning your type. The trouble is that most people don't know what group they belong to. They might work hard to convince themselves (and others) that they are a type two and that work is just that—work—but in reality, they are still looking to their jobs to complete them. Perhaps they're skeptical that it's possible to have your cake and eat it too. Or perhaps their story about what is deemed a "worthwhile career path" is clouding their judgment. Whatever the reason, these individuals often feel an itch to escape their current work reality— whether they're ready to pay attention to it or not. It may be a constant itch, or it may only surface on occasion. That itch is your inner voice nudging you to consider that there *might* be something bigger and better in store for you. If you chose your current job because it would look good on a resume or because it "made sense" as a next step at the time, but spend your days counting down the hours or complaining to friends about a boss or a coworker, you may be misclassifying yourself.

So before continuing this chapter, take a moment to honestly assess your approach to work and life: Do you view your work as one of the primary ways you can contribute to the world and others around you? Do you want or need your work to be a (or *the*) vehicle for living out your Purpose Statement—or are you not as concerned about *how* your paycheck is earned, as long as you can spend your extra time and money on activities that align with your Purpose Triggers?

As I mentioned before, one approach is not superior to the other, but becoming aware of your natural type is the first step to finding purpose at work. (Getting familiar with your inner voice will help with this too.)

Like most big life questions, there is no single answer or silver bullet for how to find meaningful work. It's going to look different for everyone, depending on your type, your Purpose Triggers, your optimal work environment, and so on. As I mentioned before, many roads lead to Rome, and hopefully you are now convinced that there is no one way to live on purpose. For some of you, pursuing your purpose may involve a career change; for others, however, it might be a matter of adopting a new perspective on work. I'm going to address both of these scenarios in this chapter.

## TAKE A BREATH

You may not appreciate this advice, but before you go looking elsewhere for more fulfilling work, try to find more purpose in the job you already have. I'm a big believer in living without "what ifs" by exhausting all possible options before calling it quits. By focusing on this as the first step, you may even discover that your dissatisfaction or lack of engagement is due to something you (or your HR team) can address; a bad boss, an overwhelming schedule, too much travel, or an obnoxious client are all solvable issues. Try to have this conversation *first* before you consider any alternatives. (I would argue that this is a good exercise for anyone to do, no matter what type you are.) More importantly, making an effort to find more meaning in the job you already have will increase the likelihood that you attract your dream gig. You don't have to be an expert on the Law of Attraction to understand that like attracts like. So, by choosing to thrive rather than survive at your current job, you are more likely to attract a new and better opportunity for yourself.

There's a famous study by three Yale professors who interviewed and observed the cleaning crew at a university hospital in an effort to understand how the custodians experienced the nature of their work. Two distinct groups emerged: the first group did not find the work particularly satisfying and, when asked to describe their responsibilities, they essentially rattled off the official job description. The second group, however, appeared to derive a great deal of purpose and satisfaction from their work. Both groups had the exact same job title, hours, and salary, so what accounted for the difference? The answer lies in something the professors defined as "job crafting": "what employees do to redesign their own jobs in ways that foster engagement at work, job satisfaction, resilience, and thriving."[10] Instead of rigidly sticking to the formal job description, the second group took it upon themselves to craft a more meaningful role: they incorporated tasks into their daily routine that weren't part of their job description; they built relationships with other staff members, patients, and their families; and they reframed their responsibilities to be more aligned with their Purpose Triggers.

This study illustrates the enormous amount of agency we have. A small shift in your mindset and attitude can make a world of difference. So, before you put in your notice or start applying to other jobs, consider (re)crafting the one you already have. You may even discover other unexpected benefits. For example, in subsequent studies, the same research team found that job crafting can lead to increased happiness at work, improved performance, and greater mobility to other roles.[11]

## HOW TO CRAFT A BETTER JOB

The first step to job crafting is getting curious. Start by asking yourself the following questions:

- Is there anything about my job that *does* excite or energize me?
- When and where do I thrive in my current role?
- What do my colleagues or clients come to me for or compliment me on most?

Then, consider how you might redesign your daily schedule and responsibilities to allocate more time to the activities that are most fulfilling to you. Similarly, consider how you might outsource some of the activities that drain or frustrate you.

If appropriate, have a conversation with your manager and share the changes you would like to propose. Make sure you focus on *why* you feel strongly about making these changes and how it will benefit your manager and the company as a whole: how will it improve your mood, your productivity, and the value you can add to the organization's mission?

The Find Your Purpose workshop was the result of my own personal recrafting. I had become borderline obsessed with personal development and felt there was an enormous opportunity to design a methodology that was more structured than the existing content (which often suggested selling all your belongings and traveling the world). During my soul-searching, I also observed that many of the job responsibilities I enjoyed the most involved one-on-one connection or facilitation in a small group setting. Instead of jumping ship to pursue these passions full-time, I had a conversation with my cofounder. She allowed me to dedicate a portion of my own and another employee's time to developing the Find Your Purpose curriculum. We built it in such a way that it could benefit many of our existing clients as well as enable us to reach a new audience, so the result was a win-win-win. I was able to scratch my personal development itch, the business had another service offering to share with clients, and we now had access to a whole new audience of individual purpose-seekers.

Beyond job crafting, here are some other suggestions that may help you find more purpose where you're at:

> **1. Start a purposeful morning routine.** Think of your mornings as a chance to set the tone for the rest of your day. If you always find yourself rushing out the door, balancing a caffeinated beverage in one hand and scrolling through your growing list of unread emails with the other, slow down. Rise and shine a little earlier so you have some wiggle room for breakfast at an actual table or for some exercise to help ground you before the daily hustle ensues. This can also be a great time to incorporate an activity related to your Purpose

Triggers, so no matter what happens throughout the rest of the day, you started it *on purpose.*

**2. Launch a side hustle.** Bill Peters defines a side hustler as a "passionate, hard-working individual who is dedicated to a sideline that provides him or her with something valuable and tangible in return, such as cash, skills, or exposure." He *almost* nailed it. The only thing missing from Peter's list of returns, in my opinion, is purpose. If you have time and energy to spare, starting a side hustle can be an excellent way to pursue your purpose alongside a nine to five job. A side hustle can not only provide an outlet for your untapped talents and passions, but it can also allow you to test ride a potential career or build a solid foundation before you decide to make it a full-time gig. My friend Tara started a coaching business while working forty hours a week at a marketing agency, for example. She started taking on a handful of clients, and eighteen months later, when her waitlist was long enough to sustain her full time, she quit.

**3. Practice purposeful time management.** Purposeful time management is a way to ensure that you are making enough time for the things that matter to you most so you can show up as your best, most passionate, creative, and compassionate self—for your work, your family, your colleagues, and your community. It enables you to prioritize your commitments or dead-lines and deliver against them, without compromising on all the other parts of yourself and your life that need to be tended to.

# THE SEVEN SECRETS OF PURPOSEFUL TIME MANAGEMENT

1. **Start your day with gratitude.** Practicing gratitude on a regular basis has been proven to increase happiness, lower cortisol levels, and even improve resilience. Just a few minutes in the morning can set you up for success, no matter what fire drills or unexpected road bumps come your way. Get in the habit of starting your day by listing three things you are grateful for. The key is not to overthink it. Your bed, a fresh cup of coffee, a lunch date later that day, the sunshine outside your window—these all count!

2. **Plan around your energy levels.** Everyone has different days of the week or times of day when they are most productive. The second step of purposeful time management is becoming aware of your own power hours so you can plan your schedule around these times. If you're a morning person, schedule your "Get Shit Done Time" first thing in the day, when you know you'll be the most focused. If you don't become a fully functioning human until after noon, leave the morning for some of the more mindless to-dos that require less of your attention. Similarly, some people are raring to go on Mondays while others need a slow start to ramp up for the work week. There's no right or wrong—it's about recognizing what works best for *you*.

3. **Check off the most important to-dos first.** Prioritizing your to-do list is critical. Start by identifying the most important task first. This is either a task that is both high in importance and high in urgency, or a task that will make all your other to-dos easier. Once you've identified this task, try to get it done as early on in your day or week as possible. This will ensure you are still fresh, and it will give you a sense of accomplishment from the get-go.

4. **Set time constraints.** A ticking clock can be one of the most effective productivity tools. Studies show that people are more productive when working under a time constraint.[12] When you have a defined period of time to get it done, you don't have the luxury of procrastinating or wasting time on indecision. According to Parkinson's Law, "Work expands so as to fill the time available for its completion." In other words, the same task can take you thirty minutes or ninety minutes, depending on how much time you allocate to it. As you plan out your day or week, set deadlines for yourself and block off slightly less time than you think you need. You may not always reach your goal, but shoot for the moon and you'll land in the stars, as they say.

5. **Focus on *one* task at a time.** Busy people are often forced to become skilled multitaskers, but you might be better off unlearning these skills. It turns out, people are much more productive when focusing on a single task at a time. This means no distractions from colleagues, kids, social media, you name it. If this sounds unrealistic for you, start with shorter blocks of time. Give yourself ten or twenty minutes to focus on one specific task and then a five-minute break to allow for those distractions. If you need a visual reminder or accountability mechanism, get yourself a

digital clock to place on your desk. For bigger tasks, break them down into smaller chunks that can be accomplished in those shorter timeframes.

As you're blocking out your time, try to group similar activities together. For example, schedule all your client calls for the week on Tuesdays and Thursdays or daily between 2:00 and 5:00 p.m., or create a whole week's worth of social content in a few hours on Monday instead of dedicating thirty minutes every day.

6. **Prioritize creative time, self-care time, and connecting time.** We need to move away from the belief that time spent on things other than work or chores on your to-do list is "unproductive." The truth is, dedicating time to being creative, caring for yourself, and connecting with others is going to make you *more* productive, not less. These activities connect you to your *why*, giving you a greater sense of purpose and drive. So make sure to proactively schedule time for these three types of activities in particular:

   • Creative time = time to brainstorm, get inspired, work through new ideas, write, read, journal, go on a walk, or whatever ignites your creative spark!

   • Self-care time = time dedicated to feeding your mind, body, and soul—this may include a workout, meditation, a warm bath, time outdoors, or whatever you need to refuel in order to show up as your best self.

   • Connecting time = time to connect with others without distraction. This may be a family dinner, coffee with a coworker, or a long-distance Skype call with an old friend.

7. **Embrace down time.** There may be moments in between scheduled blocks of time that are wide open. Try to keep some of this white space on your calendar to allow for the unexpected calls, meetings, to-dos, or other demands that will inevitably arise. On the off chance that nothing comes up, however, it's important to learn to embrace these moments instead of feeling the need to fill the gap with busywork. Take a walk, listen to music, call a friend—whatever you feel inspired to do in that moment, do it! (Your Purpose Triggers can be a great source of inspiration here too.) You may be surprised by the impact this small change can have.

## IF IT'S TIME TO MAKE MOVES

If you've exhausted your options and are still struggling to find meaning in your work, you *may* want to consider a jump. In that case, I highly recommend my brilliant friend Mike Lewis's book and podcast—both aptly titled *When to Jump*—in which he lays out a step-by-step process for taking the leap, inspired by hundreds of "Jump Stories" from people who have successfully navigated a major career change.

As you evaluate or navigate a big transition like this, consider the following advice I wish I had been given when I jumped at twenty-three.

1. **Evaluate "purpose fit."** Use your Purpose Triggers to create a personal checklist or filter for potential job opportunities. As you review a job listing, run it through your filter and determine how many of the responsibilities or activities associated with the job

align with one or more of your Purpose Triggers. Then ask yourself what you need based on your work type: is it enough for 30 percent of your day-to-day activities to be aligned with your Purpose Triggers, or are you looking for a position where the number is closer to 80 percent? This should by no means be your only evaluation criteria—things like salary, benefits, location, and growth opportunities may all be of equal importance—but it can be a helpful way to evaluate whether the opportunity is a good fit from a purpose point of view. It also helps you set more realistic expectations from the start. Just like companies assess a candidate for "culture fit," you should get in the habit of assessing a job for "purpose fit."

2.  **Communicate your wishes and expectations.** Don't be shy about communicating what's important to you and what it will take for you to thrive in a particular role. Be up front about the type of environment and work you're looking for, or what your deal breakers are—whether you're in an interview or at an informal coffee date with a mentor. Ask people who have your desired job what their day-to-day looks like and probe a little deeper to understand if or how it might line up with your Purpose Triggers.

3.  **Ask yourself: how can this job help me live out my Purpose Statement?** Better yet, grab your journal

and write it out. If it feels forced—like you're trying to make it work—that might say enough. If you can easily craft a narrative about how this particular job or career will help you live out your purpose, you're on the right track. Remember, a specific job is never the *only* way to live out your purpose—it's one of many. The answer to this question can and will change over time as your personal responsibilities shift or as the company evolves. Your dream job today may not be your dream job a decade from now—so I recommend asking yourself this question on a regular basis to ensure you're still getting what you need.

## ENTREPRENEURSHIP AND PURPOSE

Starting a new business so you can derive a greater sense of meaning from your work is the ultimate form of job crafting. As someone who took this route, I have to admit that it can be incredibly rewarding. But it's also incredibly risky. And it doesn't guarantee that you'll find purpose at the end of the rainbow—in fact, all you may find is the burden of overhead, employee management, and client retention. Moreover, as you now know, the *how* and *what* of your purpose can shift over time, and starting a business makes it even more difficult to detach your identity from this *how* or *what*.

I by no means want to deter you from pursuing your purpose through entrepreneurship. It is easily one of the best decisions I ever made, and for me, it was well worth the risk. However, if this is the path you choose, it's important to have some checks and balances in place. At least annually (preferably quarterly), ask yourself whether the business is still serving its purpose: Is your business enabling you to have your desired impact? Are you still deriving a sense of meaning from your day-to-day activities? If the answer is no, make a promise to yourself *now* that you will have the guts to listen and respond. Better yet, outline the steps you will take in the event your venture is no longer in alignment with your purpose *before* you even register your new business. Who will you share this realization with? What questions will you ask yourself? How will you evaluate whether it's a phase or something more? How might you unwind the business in a way that is the least damaging for your team, your clients, and your reputation? What would a successful exit look like? By creating a clear roadmap in advance, you are decidedly less likely to waste years on excuses as to why you can't give up on something that is no longer bringing you joy.

No matter how much you enjoy your job or how aligned it is with your purpose, there are always going to be good days and bad days. For some of us, there are good mornings and bad afternoons. Just like any successful long-term relationship or endeavor, having a fulfilling professional career requires *work*. I once asked my grandfather how he and my grandmother had managed to stay married for more than sixty-six years. He responded that it didn't feel like he had been married to the same woman for that whole time—he kept falling in love with new versions of her. Similarly, don't expect yourself to be head over heels with the same job or career forever, even if it checks all the purpose boxes. Do the work to keep falling in love with your job (and with your *why*), over and over again.

# CHAPTER TWELVE

# *RELATIONSHIPS*

> " *Life is partly what we make it, and partly what it is made by the friends we choose.* "
> —Tennessee Williams

It's easy to underestimate the importance of relationships on your journey to living a more purposeful life. Yet who we surround ourselves with has a profound impact on our sense of fulfillment and overall well-being. The longest running study on healthy aging, known as the Harvard Study of Adult Development, found that having good relationships is the single greatest predictor of long-term health and happiness. Additional benefits include lower levels of anxiety and depression, increased self-esteem, and a greater empathy for others.[13] In other words, investing in your relationships has the highest potential for return when it comes to your longevity—more than exercise, retirement savings, and professional pursuits.

The Harvard Study of Adult Development found that it isn't just *any* relationship that does the trick, however. It's *quality* relationships. How does one define quality in this context? According to the research, a "quality relationship" is one that enables you to be vulnerable, makes you feel safe, is grounded in mutual trust and understanding, and allows you to show up as your full self without fear of judgment.[14] In essence, it's those pack-worthy relationships that have the greatest potential to guarantee our life satisfaction as a centenarian.

Building quality relationships requires a great degree of intentionality. It requires us to be deliberate about how we choose to allocate our most precious assets—our time and our energy—so we can cultivate connections that add greater meaning (and more years) to our lives. People can either bring out the best *or* the worst in us, and when you're on a mission to live on purpose, you can't afford to have anyone bringing you down. Fortunately, for the most part, we get to choose which relationships we invest in. We also get to choose *how* we prefer to develop these connections. Just as it is important to cultivate self-awareness around what your needs are from a professional point of view, the same is true for your social life.

## EMBRACE YOUR PREFERENCES

A lot of people think my husband is an extrovert. When he is "on," he's the life of the party, the ultimate instigator, and the last one standing on any dance floor. What many don't know, however, is that he will need the next day to recharge—ideally by himself, on the couch, with a good audiobook. We joke that he's either a zero or a one. I, on the other hand, am always operating at a steady 0.5. Everything in moderation might as well be my middle name. While he is corralling the party guests to play another game, I'm sneaking up to bed or in the kitchen having a deep personal conversation with another guest. But while he's hibernating on the couch the next day, I'm out meeting friends for lunch. Once again, the point is that it's okay to embrace your true nature. In fact, it's more than okay—it's imperative. Relationships are another instance in which many people succumb to the slippery slope of "shoulds": I "should" be friends with my coworkers, I "should" host the other parents for a dinner party, I "should" be attending that networking event.

If you're an introvert who prefers one-on-one coffee dates to dinner parties, save yourself the agony and stick to coffee. If you're an extrovert who thrives in large group settings, by all means say a *hell yes* to becoming the local charity's new social chair. Remember that your *only* job is to design a life that lights you up—this includes the way you socialize.

## THE LIFE-CHANGING MAGIC OF KONMARI-ING YOUR FRIENDS

Like its author, the bestselling book *The Life-Changing Magic of Tidying Up* is small but mighty. It packs a punch. Japanese decluttering expert Marie Kondo made more than a splash with her KonMari Method, which even inspired a Netflix series. Her method is grounded in centuries of Japanese wisdom and, given this origin story, it's not surprising that the method's magic lies in its simplicity. It all comes down to a single question: "Does it spark joy?" Marie teaches her readers how to use this question to eliminate any unnecessary or uninspiring items from their homes. After reading this book, I KonMaried our entire house over the course of a weekend. To my husband's delight, I decluttered our closets, the kitchen cabinets, my office, and pretty much every storage space in our house. To any skeptics out there, I can honestly say from experience that this book lives up to its audacious title: it really is *life-changing*. I felt lighter and calmer, and every time I open a well-organized cabinet, I still feel highly accomplished.

I was hooked. I became addicted to getting rid of anything superfluous and started thinking about how I could apply this same framework to other areas of my life: my to-do list, my calendar, and even my friendships. That's right, I KonMaried my relationships. Now before you jump to conclusions about what an awful person I am, please know I didn't actually *break up* with friends that didn't spark joy. We're talking about people here—not plants—so there's obviously a limit to how ruthless one can be. But a lot can be learned from the basic KonMari principles.

We make and keep friends for many different reasons: shared interests, kids of similar ages, proximity, convenience, mutual connections, obligation, and guilt, just to name a few. Not all of these reasons are equally valid (or healthy, for that matter). So I assessed all the relationships in my life and started asking myself: Do I enjoy spending time with this person? Do I look forward to hearing from them? Do I feel more energized and excited about things after I speak to them? I had some very clear "yes" and "no" answers, as well as a lot of "maybes." This is not about awakening your inner Mean Girl. It's not about ending relationships overnight or agonizing over your "maybes"—it's about doubling down on the clear "yeses" and making sure you're investing the majority of your time and energy in those relationships. By intentionally surrounding yourself with quality connections—with the people who spark joy—you will show up as a better, more purpose-driven version of yourself.

## HOW TO KONMARI YOUR FRIENDSHIPS

Make a list of all the people in your life. (I found it helpful to use my phone contacts for this.) Then work your way down the list and ask yourself:

- Do I enjoy spending time with this person?
- Do I look forward to hearing from them?
- Do I feel more energized and excited about things after I see or hear from them?

Make a commitment to prioritize the people who got a hell yes on all three questions. Especially if these individuals aren't as present in your life as you'd like them to be. Send them a text or an email—or better yet, give them a call. You might even consider making them part of your pack. For advice on how to invest in these relationships further, revisit Purpose Enabler #2 in chapter 10.

While I am not advocating you cut any people out of your life, it may be worth spending some time reviewing your "nos" as well. How much time are you spending with these people today? Coming back to one of our Purpose Blockers, sometimes your biggest critics can be disguised as your best friends.

# CHAPTER THIRTEEN

# *PLAY*

> "*You can discover more about a person in an hour of play than an hour of conversation.*"
> —Plato

Like many ex-consultants, I am a recovering results-oholic. As such, it should come as no surprise to anyone that "play" has been the hardest purpose pistachio for me crack. For so many years, it felt frivolous to me. If I'm being completely honest, I would even venture to say that it felt like a waste of time. I had somehow convinced myself that everything I did *had* to have a tangible outcome: a box I could check or a final deliverable I could point to. I took pride in dedicating every hour of my day to something "productive." If you were a client, a business partner, or a colleague of mine, this character flaw was greatly appreciated. I was reliable and typically couldn't help but over-deliver. If you were a close friend or my husband, however, it was exhausting. I could watch TV for a whole thirty minutes before I would start to get restless. On Sunday mornings my poor husband had to bribe me to stay in bed instead of running off to an 8:00 a.m. workout class, because lying in felt too self-indulgent to me. It took me *years* to learn that the whole purpose of play is that *it has no purpose*. It's not about the result but about the experience itself. That's exactly why it's so powerful.

## NIX THE DOUBLE STANDARD

Play is highly encouraged in children. In fact, several famous psychologists (including Freud) suggest that play is essential to a child's development. Researchers study children's play to learn more about what drives the individual child, as well as how he or she processes information, solves problems, and interacts with the world around them. A lot of important lessons are disguised in the form of play, and it has the ability to increase both creative capacity and interpersonal skills. So given all of its superpowers, why do we start to neglect (and even discredit) play as we become adults? Do we grow out of our *need* to play? Do we become immune to the benefits? Nope. While play may not serve the same developmental functions as it does in early childhood, it still has a lot of positive side effects in adults. In addition to releasing endorphins, stimulating creativity, and improving our overall brain health, play also has the potential to reduce our sensitivity to stressors.[15] The more playful you are, the less likely you are to succumb to stress. Given the number of adults who are operating under severe stress and the impact this has on our collective health and well-being, play has the potential to make a huge difference in our lives. Beyond its calming effects, however, the reason I have become such a raving fan of play is because of its connection to purpose: play is one of the most obvious breadcrumbs when searching for your sweet spot. Play is a great way to remind you of your *why*.

When you play, you lose sense of space and time—you become spellbound by the present moment. You let go of any expectations and let yourself be led by what truly engages, entertains, or excites you. It follows that the activities you are drawn to as play—both as a child and an adult—are excellent indications of your Purpose Triggers. So ask yourself: What do you do just for fun—with no other motives in mind? What do you do purely for pleasure? For some of you, the better question might be: Do you even make time for *anything* that is purely for pleasure? Your answers are full of clues indicating your preferred form of play.

Here are some of my personal favorite ways to play:

Cooking (especially when listening to any type of jazz music)
Dancing or moving my body in any way
Singing
Writing
Listening to podcasts while walking around my neighborhood

These preferences may change over time, and I am by no means suggesting that I am *always* in the mood to cook or dance. But, when I *do* make the time, these activities enable me to become fully absorbed in the moment. So much so, that I let go of the outcome entirely. I do these things purely because it feels good—not because they're productive. I've learned, in time, that that is a perfectly acceptable reason.

## SCHEDULE MORE PLAYDATES

Take some time to figure out what your favorite acts of play are. Revisit your answer to Discovery Mission #10 and consider the questions posed here:

- What do you do just for fun—with no other motives in mind?

- If you had an entire weekend to yourself—no people to please, no work to do, no errands to run—how would you spend it?

Remember that this is still a judgement-free zone—don't prematurely discount what comes up or respond with an activity you *wish* you wanted to do. You might love the *idea* of being a yogi, but if seventy-five minutes of breath-to-movement still feels like torture after months of trying, it's not considered play. At least not for you. Play should feel effortless and, you guessed it, playful.

Once you have identified your preferred act(s) of play, be intentional about making time for these activities. Unfortunately, "playtime" or "recess" is no longer featured on the average adult's calendar. But it should be. Of course, there will always be a pile of excuses you can bury yourself under, including "I'm too busy," "I'm too tired," and "I'm not feeling well." These stories will feel all the more legitimate when it comes to play because there's nothing at stake—no deadlines or people depending on you to get it done. Ah, but that's where you're wrong. There *is* something at stake: your path to purpose. Play is *not* a waste of time. Pursuing these breadcrumbs is a critical part of this journey because it will lead you to one of the most important clues: *What are you drawn to do when no one is watching (or judging) you?*

# SCHEDULE A PLAYDATE WITH YOURSELF

Your homework assignment is to pencil in time for a weekly playdate with yourself. Whatever you do, don't take a rain check when other "more important things" come up. Because nothing is more important than filling your purpose cup.

So how do you prioritize play in a world that doesn't give it the respect it deserves? Stop taking yourself and the outcome so seriously. When you make this shift, you will start to notice a positive impact on all areas of your life. (I speak from experience here.) If you're still struggling to identify your own preferred method of play, here are a few suggestions to get started[16]:

- **Crack open an adult coloring book.** Even if you don't consider yourself "artsy," this can be surprisingly fun and relaxing all at once. Remember, it's not about the outcome, so coloring outside the lines is encouraged.

- **Wander: go for a walk or a bike ride without a destination in mind.** Leave your phone at home (or put it in airplane mode) and set out into the wild unknown. Live on the edge— who knows what you might discover!

- **Try a new-to-you activity.** You don't have to be good at something to enjoy it. Bake a new recipe, sign up for a ceramics class, or go to your local rock-climbing wall. Let go of any expectations and just enjoy!

- **Get your hands dirty.** Do you remember the days when a little bit of soil, paint, or sand didn't faze you? Perhaps it was even a badge of honor—the dirtier, the better. Build a sandcastle at the beach, roll up your sleeves in the garden, or dip your feet in a local creek. Stop worrying about the laundry you'll have to do or the sand that will inevitably get all over your house—the benefits of play are well worth a little mess.

- **Embrace your inner gamer.** Games—whether they're played on a board with friends or virtually—can stimulate your mind in ways that your daily routine cannot. It's not about the competition (although it can be); it's about losing yourself in an activity that serves no other purpose than to entertain.

# CHAPTER FOURTEEN

# *MONEY*

> "You can only become truly accomplished
> at something you love. Don't make money
> your goal. Instead, pursue the things you
> love doing, and then do them so well that
> people can't take their eyes off you."
> —Maya Angelou

The only topic that is more taboo than politics and sex is money. Beyond being the leading cause of societal plagues such as divorce and stress, it is also one of the most common excuses people use to avoid pursuing their purpose: "I can't *afford* to leave my job . . . to start a company . . . to take a pay cut . . . to invest in myself right now." While these excuses may sound justifiable, they aren't serving you. All they're serving is the story inside your head. Moreover, if you ascribe to the philosophy that like attracts like, you are not doing yourself any favors. The more you blame money, the bigger an obstacle it will become; the more you talk about how little you have, the less you will end up with.

When it comes to money and purpose, there's a lot to unpack, but it starts with understanding your own money story. If asked to define our relationship with money on Facebook, the majority of us would select "It's Complicated." So the first step to purposeful money management is simplifying the situation by acknowledging your own money story: the beliefs you've picked up over the course of your life that have come to shape your relationship to money. We all have them—whether your primary caregivers growing up lived paycheck to paycheck or in an environment of financial abundance. I am by no means minimizing the harsh realities that accompany financial hardship—however, the trick is not to wallow in your financial fate, but rather to reframe your money mindset to work *for* you instead of against you. Once again, it comes down to focusing on the factors you *can* control. In this chapter, I will outline four of the money mindset shifts that transformed my relationship with my bank account.

## UNCOVER YOUR MONEY STORIES

Here are some questions to help you discover what conscious and unconscious beliefs you have adopted about money. I suggest taking some time to write your responses in your journal.

- What did you learn from your parents or primary caregivers about money? What did they model?
- What is your first memory about *earning* money?
- What is your first memory about *receiving* money as a gift?
- How do you feel when you donate money?
- Do you have a scarcity mindset ("there's never enough") or an abundance mindset ("there's always more to be had")? Where did that come from?
- What are your greatest fears about money?
- What would a healthy relationship with money look like?

Now that you have a better understanding of what your limiting beliefs are and how you might have gotten them, it's time to reframe your relationship with money.

## *MINDSET SHIFT #1*
### THERE IS ALWAYS ENOUGH MONEY TO LIVE ON PURPOSE

You cannot live on purpose when you're stuck in a scarcity mindset. If you're constantly obsessing over what you lack, instead of being grateful for what you do have, you're operating from scarcity. Some of the happiest and most fulfilled people on earth live on less than a dollar a day, so while there are obvious disadvantages to financial hardship, it by no means excludes you from finding (and staying on) your highlighted route.

In 2016, a group of researchers published a study demonstrating that people who feel a greater sense of purpose are more likely to accumulate wealth (and maintain that wealth over time) compared to those who lack a sense of meaning in life.[17] This held true even when they controlled for other factors such as socioeconomic status and personality traits. While it is difficult to attribute the participants' income levels to purpose alone, the correlation is noteworthy. Here is my interpretation of the data: If you are pursuing your purpose, you are deserving of abundance. Period. Because when you're operating in service of something greater than yourself, the universe will show up to support you. It will provide whatever your purpose seed requires to grow and mature—whether it be money, a public platform, or a compatible business partner.

Take Emily, for example, one of our workshop students. Through the Find Your Purpose process, she discovered that what she really wanted to do with her life was open a yoga studio. At the time, she was working as a paralegal at a top law firm. After working through all her Purpose Blockers—and there were quite a few, as you can imagine—the only thing still holding her back was money. She would have to commit to a long-term lease and invest quite a bit of capital to transform the space into the oasis she envisioned. Fortunately, Emily didn't let this final hurdle stop her. She continued to follow the Purpose Plan framework which you will learn about in chapter 15 and asked herself: what is the *next* best step? In her case, she decided to open a pop-up studio and teach a few classes a week after work. This led her to meet her business partner, who happened to have a perfectly complementary skill set and shared Emily's vision. Within a few months, their classes were packed, and students were begging the duo to do more. That's when their first investor reached out, and within a matter of months they were able to raise sufficient funds to lease a permanent space. Today, Emily runs a successful small business. The studio is not only wildly popular with local yogis, but she added another revenue stream by inviting brands to host events and photo shoots in the space. If Emily hadn't taken that first step—if she hadn't bet on herself and her dream—the investor would have most likely never have materialized. Giant leaps happen one small step at a time, so don't worry too much about the *how* and stay fiercely committed to your *why*.

As long as your intentions are pure—as long as the "why" is aligned with your purpose—you'll be surprised at how quickly you might attract the capital or the partners you need. Notice that I said pure, *not* saintly. There is absolutely no need to feel guilty about spending money on yourself and your family, as long as it's for the right reason. In fact, someone who donates their entire life savings to charity, but does so begrudgingly or in an effort to impress their social circles, may be worse off than someone who spends all their money on a new Lamborghini. If the second individual is crazy passionate about cars—perhaps even considers them to be a Purpose Trigger—this investment may be exactly what that person needs to show up as a better friend, parent, colleague, partner, and neighbor to those around them.

## *MINDSET SHIFT #2*
### THERE IS NO MAGIC NUMBER

A lot of people—particularly those who are stuck in a scarcity mindset—view money as a form of salvation. *If I only had a million dollars*, I would never be stressed; I would pursue my dreams; I would save for retirement; etc. The problem is that as soon as you reach a million dollars, you start dreaming of all the things you could do with two million or five million, and so on. This "if only" approach to money (and life more generally) can be dangerous because it can cause you to lose sight of what really matters. If you are solely motivated by money, you will never have enough, and you will never be content. As long as you view money as the solution to your problems, you are actively giving your power away. You're positioning yourself as a victim who is incapable of solving their own challenges through resourcefulness. A fixation on money can also become a distraction from the deeper, more uncomfortable truths you are running away from. Money may reduce stress temporarily, but you will soon find new things to stress about. You will eventually discover that the root cause of the anxiety was never the status of your bank account to begin with.

The best way to determine if you're relying too much on money to make you happy is by asking yourself the magic three-letter word: Why? Why do you want to accept a job offer? Why is it so important to make a particular investment or reach a specific revenue goal? In other words, are you chasing financial success so you can live in closer alignment to your true self or because you're trying to prove something or meet someone's expectations? If you're motivated by any reason other than your desire to live out your best, most purpose-driven life, you're setting yourself up for grave disappointment. I'm not saying you won't be wealthy because you very well might be. But you will eventually learn that the rumors are true: money doesn't buy happiness. It can buy opportunity, it can buy distraction, and it may be able to buy you time—but it cannot buy fulfillment. Fulfillment doesn't cost a thing—as long as you're willing to do the work outlined in these chapters.

So, instead of letting an arbitrary number define how you feel about yourself, step into your own worth *before* your net worth reflects it. Trust that your self-worth will translate into your net worth, not the other way around. Before you set your next financial goal, take a moment to reflect on your why. Be specific about the opportunity you want to create for yourself and how the cash or investment will help you live in greater alignment with your purpose. Like any tool, money can be used as a force for good or evil, depending on the owner's intention. With the right intention, money can indeed accelerate your journey to purpose and provide a tremendous amount of freedom. Without a clear intention, however, it isn't nearly as powerful.

# MINDSET SHIFT #3

## INVEST FOR THE HIGHEST ROI

Ramit Sethi is the brains behind the concept of "Money Dials." Think of Money Dials as your financial Purpose Triggers: the things you spend on that bring you an inordinate amount of joy. According to Sethi, the ten most common Money Dials are convenience, travel, health and fitness, experiences, freedom, relationships, generosity, luxury, social status, and self-improvement. Of course, we all enjoy spending money in several of these categories, but each of us has *one* dial to rule them all. One thing we *love* to spend on more than anything else. It varies from person to person. (I'm sure there have been plenty of instances in which you wondered why on earth your friends spend their hard-earned cash the way they do.)

For example, my husband's money dial is convenience. Every time we drive to LAX airport, he insists on paying a premium for a fancy valet service so we don't have to bother with the long-term parking shuttle. This feels like a highly unnecessary luxury to me—I was almost too embarrassed to share it here—but to my husband, the added convenience is well worth the additional twenty dollars a day. On the flip side, he cannot wrap his head around my willingness to spend six dollars on an overpriced latte when you can get a perfectly decent cup of joe at any corner store for a dollar. Learning about Money Dials has helped us develop a whole new understanding and appreciation for each other's preferences on the spending front.

The point is not to judge your own or other people's Money Dials; it's to become aware of what type of expenditures give you the greatest return on your investment. For some, living in a smaller city to save on rent so they can take a whole month off to travel each year is well worth it, while others wouldn't dream of living anywhere but New York or Los Angeles, where they can attend the hottest social events. Once you get clear on what this is for you, it becomes a lot easier to spend with purpose.

Ask yourself which of the following Money Dials is number one for you:

Convenience
Travel
Health and fitness
Experiences
Freedom
Relationships
Generosity
Luxury
Social status
Self-improvement

Now look at your spending patterns and see if you may be able to reduce your spending in other categories in order to allocate more of your available funds to the things that offer you the greatest return in the form of joy and purpose.

## *MINDSET SHIFT #4*
## DON'T PUT PRESSURE ON YOUR
## PURPOSE TO PAY THE BILLS

Remember that work is not the *only* way to find meaning in life. In fact, most people find it elsewhere—in relationships, play, or philanthropy, just to name a few sources of purpose. Your purpose is so much bigger than your business card or your pay stub. Author Elizabeth Gilbert, who sold over ten million copies of her travel memoir *Eat, Pray, Love,* was all too aware of this trap. She stubbornly kept her day job for years, even though she was making good money as a writer. In her book *Big Magic,* she says, "I never wanted to burden my creativity with the task of providing for me in the material world." Now this by no means applies to *all* people—in some cases, your sweet spot can indeed provide for you—but it's important to take the pressure off.

I love to sing. As a young girl, I would lock myself in a room for hours on end and sing along with every Broadway soundtrack I could get my hands on. I took the four-hour round-trip journey to the south of Holland every Saturday to be part of a prestigious musical theatre program, and for a while, I seriously considered pursuing it as a profession. That's how much I loved it. So what happened? Well, I pictured my life as a full-time performer and played it out in great detail. I would be on stage seven nights a week (including holidays), I would have very little control over my schedule, I would live out of a suitcase, and I would be surrounded by a new cast of characters every few months. This might sound like a dream to some of you, but it wasn't the lifestyle I knew would make me happy. I need to feel grounded, and I love my routines. More importantly, however, I realized that what singing really was to me was an escape—a way to get lost in the moment and let go of whatever else might be going on in my life. What would happen if my escape became my livelihood, I asked myself? The answer, of course, was that it would no longer bring me the same amount of joy it once did. I wasn't willing to make that sacrifice.

If you expect (or force) every Purpose Trigger to turn into an income stream, those triggers will quickly lose their luster. Accept that you can still live a wildly purposeful life without earning a living from your purpose.

The key takeaway from this chapter is that money is not an end goal in and of itself—it's a means to an end. Moreover, wealth is not a specific number, it's a mindset. Money has no meaning unless you make it mean something, and it cannot lead to fulfillment unless you invest the available funds in what matters most *to you*. There is more than enough money in the world for all seven billion of us to live on purpose, so stop using it as an excuse to put your dreams on hold, and start to trust that you will receive whatever it is that you need, if (or when) you decide to pump up the volume.

# *A ROADMAP TO LIVING YOUR BEST LIFE*

As I mentioned at the beginning of Part Three, it's not enough to *know* your purpose. To truly transform your life and live *on purpose*, you have to take action—and you have to take action consistently. Like any practice—including athletic endeavors, playing an instrument, and meditation—consistency is far more important than the scope of any one of your actions. There's no such thing as baby steps in this case. Your steps can be as big or as small as you need them to be, as long as they are frequent and represent a *forward* motion—in the direction of your highlighted route.

A subtle but important distinction between a vocation or a skill and a *practice* is that a practice always leaves room for growth. You are never done learning—no matter how many hours you dedicate to your activity of choice. Part of this is driven by the dynamic nature of human beings. Your external and internal environments are always in motion. As a result, you will never approach a practice from the same starting point. You may effortlessly access your inner voice some days, only to struggle to tap into that inner well of wisdom the next. You may be in the midst of a major life transition one year, only to feel stagnant and stuck the next. But it's not a matter of *if* or *when* you will get derailed from your highlighted route—because this *will* happen at some point, no matter how en-lightened you are. What matters is how quickly you can recognize a detour for what it is and course-correct to find your way back into alignment. The secret to a fulfilling life is constant (re)orientation toward your purpose.

While a practice will always require a certain degree of effort and investment, it *can* get easier. The more you anticipate or recog-nize Purpose Blockers and the more automatic it becomes to draw on your favorite Purpose Enablers, the smoother the journey will be. Just like training any muscle or building any new habit, consis-tent action over time will enable you to override old conditioning and replace it with a new pattern. Every time you dance with fear, you'll get a little more comfortable being uncomfortable. Every time you choose forgiveness over guilt, you will love yourself a lit-tle more. Every time you turn inward for encouragement instead of searching for external validation, you will become stronger. Culti-vating the practice of living on purpose is a lifelong pursuit, but it does not have to take a lifetime to start experiencing benefits. All it takes is one choice. The moment you choose to be the victor of your story instead of the victim. The moment you choose purpose over any number of alternatives. Following the law of momentum, the more of these decisions you can string together, the more pow-erful your internal compass will become and the less effort it will require to live on purpose.

## YOUR PURPOSE PLAN

The consultant in me couldn't bear the thought of leaving you high and dry without a framework for this final part of the process. So I would like to introduce you to your new best friend: your Purpose Plan. Think of your Purpose Plan as your personal roadmap to purpose. If your Purpose Statement describes your *why*, your Purpose Plan describes your *how*. It is designed to help you infuse more meaning into every dimension of your life: your career, your relationships, your leisure time, and your financials. Drawing on the data points you have collected thus far, you will come up with a set of concrete goals for incorporating more Purpose Triggers into every dimension of your life, as well as outline the action steps required to achieve each goal. Your purpose journey is a marathon, not a sprint, and your Purpose Plan is designed to support this type of gradual transformation. Your Purpose Plan will help you break down bigger goals into manageable steps and create systems to hold you accountable for making progress against them.

I can't emphasize enough the importance of having a plan—whether it's a plan to pursue your purpose or any other endeavor for that matter. A plan offers three primary benefits to purpose-seekers. First, it reduces the likelihood that you get distracted. You know exactly where you're going and what needs to happen in order to get there. This clarity can empower you to say "no" more readily to anything that might derail you from your highlighted route. It reminds you of the bigger picture—your North Star—and acts as an anchor when you are at risk of drifting off. Second, it avoids overwhelm. One of the most common blocks I hear people talk about at the outset of this journey is that there are *too many* options. A good plan will clearly outline what your next step is, so you don't become paralyzed by all the potential paths that are available to you. Finally, the plan gives you the opportunity to practice Purpose Enabler #3: self-discipline. Every time you complete one step of your Purpose Plan, you become a little more confident in your ability to tackle the next one, and then the next—until your track record is so solid that you don't question whether you're capable anymore.

The Purpose Plan is designed around the next best step because it's the only step that really matters. I almost didn't write this book because I was so intimidated by having to build a platform and promote myself. This is step number fifty, however, not step number one. More often than not, you'll find that when you get to step forty-nine, step fifty will seem much less scary than it did when you were at the beginning of your journey. So instead of fixating on what will be required from you in the future, your Purpose Plan focuses all your attention on what is required from you *in the present* in order to take meaningful action.

You can use the template in this book or go to www.purpose-playbook.com/purposeplan to download a printable version. I recommend doing this exercise once a month for *at least* three consecutive months if you want to increase the likelihood that your changes stick. The data varies, but most researchers agree that it takes anywhere between sixty to ninety days to form a new habit, and we don't want to take any risks when something as important as your potential to live on purpose is at stake.

Here are the four steps for building and using your Purpose Plan:

1. **Identify the *one* thing.** For each dimension, come up with *one* thing you can do to start incorporating your Purpose Triggers into that particular area of your life.

   *For example, if my first Purpose Trigger is "teaching and developing others," I might choose the following strategies:*

   > **Work:** Mentor a younger team member.
   >
   > **Relationships:** Share a list of my favorite personal development books with my tribe.
   >
   > **Play:** Read *Anatomy of Yoga* in order to improve my own practice and teaching.
   >
   > **Money:** Write a blog post about what I've learned about purposeful money management (and the mistakes I made along the way).

   When defining your *one* thing, remember:

   - **Make it as specific as possible.** No action is too small or insignificant.

   - **Make it realistic.** Choose something you know you can achieve if you set your mind to it. That being said, your goals should feel slightly uncomfortable because the real magic happens outside your comfort zone, after all.

   - **Make it self-sufficient.** Choose a goal that is not dependent on external factors or other people. Don't let something or someone outside your control derail your journey.

2.  **Describe the next best step.** Now, break it down even further. For each of the goals you identified, describe the next best step you need to take in order to make progress toward your goal. Choose an action you can commit to completing in the next thirty days.

    - **Work:** Mentor a younger team member.
        » Action: Reach out to a younger team member who I feel I can help and schedule a coffee date.

    - **Relationships:** Share a list of my favorite personal development books with my tribe.
        » Action: Compile a list of my favorite personal development books and a one-line description for why I love each of them.

    - **Play:** Read *Anatomy of Yoga* in order to improve my own practice and teaching.
        » Action: Purchase *Anatomy of Yoga*.

    - **Money:** Write a blog post on what I've learned about purposeful money management (and the mistakes I made along the way).
        » Action: Create an outline for the blog post by listing the top five things I've learned about purposeful money management.

3. **Hold yourself accountable.** To ensure that you are following through on your Purpose Plan, I recommend doing one or all of the following:

- Identify an accountability partner and share your goals and action steps with them. Schedule a call or in-person date for roughly a month from today and ask them to check in with you on your progress at that time.

- Block off an hour on your calendar thirty days from now and title the meeting: "Purpose Plan Review." Use this time to take yourself on an accountability date to reflect on your progress in each dimension. Be honest about where you're at and ask yourself the following questions:

  » Did I complete my next best step?

  » If not, why not? Am I still working through some resistance in this dimension? Was my next best step specific, realistic, and self-sufficient enough? What can I do better next month?

  » If yes, what is something that worked well that I can apply in the future?

  » How has this small step forward impacted my sense of fulfillment?

- Read *Atomic Habits* by James Clear. This book brilliantly outlines how to systematically design your routines to support healthy habit formation.

4. **Rinse and repeat.** In thirty days, repeat steps two and three again. Based on the progress you've made against your goals to date, what is the *next* best step? If you didn't complete your action step in the last thirty days, you may want to keep it as is for that particular dimension—or you may choose to update it to something that feels more doable.

Continue this pattern until you have achieved your goals. Then, determine whether you would like to set new goals for each Purpose Trigger or focus on cultivating daily routines and habits that will help you stay aligned.

## THINK LIKE A MARKETER

Any marketer knows that a new sale can rarely be attributed to a single channel or campaign. More often than not, prospective buyers are influenced by multiple touch points. An online advertisement, a friend's recommendation, an in-store display—these small nudges add up, and every encounter increases the likelihood that the prospect becomes an actual customer.

It can be helpful to approach your path to purpose in a similar fashion. To increase the likelihood that you will continue to reorient yourself toward your highlighted route, set up a system of multiple touch points.

Here are some suggestions, based on other exercises included in this book:

• Print multiple copies of your Purpose Plan and place them somewhere visible to you: your fridge, your desk, your bathroom mirror, your bedside table, or on the inside of your closet door.

- Do the same with your Purpose Statement: create a note on your phone, write it on the first page of your journal, make a screensaver of your statement, or get creative with arts and crafts. Whenever you're facing a decision or debating whether or not to say yes to something, run it through this filter: Will this allow me to live in greater alignment with my Purpose Statement? If so, make it a *hell yes*.

- Keep multiple journals so there's never an excuse not to write it out. Personally, I keep one next to my bed and one in my work bag.

- Sprinkle little reminders, quotes, and other words of encouragement around your house on stickies or create a dedicated bulletin board (physical or digital) for them. You may not notice these most days, but they will be there when you need a little extra TLC. Some of my favorite one-liners from this book include:
  - » "Other people's opinion is none of your business." —Robin Sharma
  - » Focus on my fans.
  - » All purpose *is* created equal.
  - » Put my own oxygen mask on first before helping others.
  - » Fear is an illusion. *What if* I was fearless?
  - » Does this person or activity fill my cup?
  - » Have I played today?

Remember, you have to be your own biggest cheerleader. Waiting for someone else to hold your hand or serve you your purpose on a silver platter is a waste of time. You already know who you're meant to be. In fact, you're the *only* person who knows. All you have to do is pay attention to the clues and take inspired action— one step at a time.

## TIME TO TAKE THE WHEEL

As Howard Thurman so beautifully articulated, the world *needs* you to come alive. We *need* you to show up and become the person you were meant to be. I know it's scary. I know it's overwhelming. I know it's uncomfortable. But guess what? Those are all prerequisites for growth. And what is the point of life if not to evolve and grow? Every day is another opportunity for you to step a little closer to your highest potential. Besides, what do you have to lose? While you may be conditioned to think otherwise, life is meant to be *enjoyed*, not *endured*. The approach you choose is ultimately up to you. The reason I felt so compelled to write this book is because I've met too many people who have yet to internalize this truth. They are idly waiting for opportunities to miraculously appear on their path, instead of taking control of their own happy ending. You are the author of your life story. You are the driver of your imaginary vehicle. So take the frickin' wheel and stop being a passenger in your own life. Stop settling.

I hope this book has given you greater clarity on what matters to you most and how you can engineer your reality to live on purpose. No magic wands, crystals, or psychics necessary (although all are welcome, of course). What *is* essential, however, is an unwavering foundation of trust. Trust that you *do* have a purpose. Trust that you *know* what that purpose is—even if it's buried underneath layers of conditioning and stories. Finally, trust that the more you lean into your purpose, the more the universe will show up to support you.

This is not a one-and-done type of adventure. My objective for writing this book was to help you access your personal GPS and equip you with a set of navigational tools so you can continue to find your way back to the highlighted route, time and time again. Before you set off on your purpose quest, I want to summarize several of the most important lessons I hope you take away from this book:

1. **You (and only you) are responsible for giving your life meaning.** If you do *one* thing with your time on earth, let it be (re)aligning yourself with your purpose. No one can (or will) do the work for you, so take responsibility. What you get *out* of life is directly proportional to what you invest *in* it. If you continue to play small and avoid showing up fully for your gifts and for your purpose, life will never show up fully to support you. You will never experience what it's like to live *on purpose* and become the full expression of who you were meant to be.

2. **The secret to finding your purpose is following the clues (aka Purpose Triggers).** What it ultimately

boils down to is this: do what brings you joy. Operate in your sweet spot as much as possible. You may think that "everyone" enjoys your passion for reading historical fiction or candle making as much as you do, but you're wrong. You were given certain gifts and interests for a reason, so lean into what lights you up. This doesn't mean you should quit your job to pursue candle making for a living, but it *does* mean that you should stop viewing candle making as any less of a priority than your nine to five. In fact, dedicating more time to candle making may actually *increase* your productivity at work and greatly improve your relationships with friends and family. The goal is to design your life in such a way that you are constantly filling your cup so you can contribute your gifts to others.

3. **All purpose is created equal.** No purpose is more or less worthy than another. It is essential that every individual embraces their unique purpose. Think about our planet, for example—its future depends on the biodiversity of life on earth. Every species has a specific role to play, thereby contributing to the richness of our ecosystem. If one species becomes extinct or fails to fulfill its duties, the planet becomes more susceptible to threats like climate change. Similarly, for humans to thrive—spiritually, physically, and emotionally—it is imperative that each of us pursue our *own* path to purpose. If we continue to ignore our inner compass

and blindly follow the car in front of us, we are dragging the collective down.

4.  **Purpose doesn't have to pay the bills.** Not everyone can make a living off of their purpose, nor should everyone *want* to. Remember that your purpose is bigger than any one job. If you remain fixated on making your profession your purpose, you may miss out on a myriad of other ways to find joy. We are conditioned to place too much value on what we *do*—what our lives look like *on paper*. But at the end of the day, when we take our final breath, the only thing that counts is who we *are*. Our legacy consists of so much more than our professional contributions—it consists of the way we showed up for ourselves, for our lives, and for others.

5.  **Nature doesn't make mistakes.** Trust your curiosities and give yourself permission to pursue them. What lights you up is a clue about what you're meant to do. Accept that however well-intentioned your parents, teachers, and colleagues may be, they will often project their own fears and stories onto you. Be brave enough to be honest with yourself: What are *your* true Purpose Triggers versus the Triggers you chase because it impresses or pleases others? Embrace opportunities to zig when others zag, as it's a clear signal that you're moving in the right direction. The beauty of the highlighted route is that it is always there. It is always

just one decision or reframe away. No matter how many wrong turns you've taken or how far off course you get, you can always find your way back. Purpose is never a lost cause.

6. **You are enough, just the way you are.** As long as you're chasing someone else's purpose or someone else's dream, you will never be fulfilled. There will always be an emptiness inside you, no matter how hard you try to fill it with any number of anesthetics—drugs, alcohol, social media, or professional achievement. The only path to true fulfillment is identifying and pursuing your own, one-of-a-kind path. Live an unfiltered life.

All that is left to do now is to invite you to join me on this mission. I invite you to commit to following the clues and taking action in accordance with them. I invite you to come alive and become the person you were meant to be. This mission is so much greater than you or I. When we live in alignment with our purpose, we inspire others to do the same. Forgive the new age prose, but just imagine how much more "high vibe" the world would be if people had permission to do what truly brings them joy, instead of forcing themselves to run in a race that was never theirs to compete in—or squeeze their foot into a shoe that's too small.

So how do you know when you're on the highlighted route? What does it feel like to live on purpose—to be operating in your sweet spot more often than not? In my experience, one of the most telling signs was a dramatic shift in the way I perceived and measured time. When I was a management consultant, I knew exactly how many weeks were left until the end of a project, a big social event, or my next weekend getaway. I was always counting down the days to *something*. I was so focused on the next milestone that the time in between passed as if I were in a daze. I would go through the motions—day in, day out—until the event or celebration finally arrived, only to start the countdown all over again. It was a coping mechanism—a way to distract my purpose-seeking soul from the purposeless monotony of my daily grind.

It wasn't until a few months after my jump that I noticed the change. I no longer looked forward to a far-off date in the future. I was so passionate about what I was doing that it consumed me entirely. I couldn't comprehend where I would be or what I would be working on in a week, let alone a month or two from now. If anything, there weren't enough hours in the day to check off the items on my never-ending to-do list. The future could wait! Whereas I used to dread late nights and weekends in the office, I now looked forward to them. I would practically skip to our coworking space on Saturday mornings and have to force myself to leave when it was time to meet my friends for dinner. Seven years later, I may no longer be as enthusiastic about weekend work, but I am still living moment to moment instead of milestone to milestone. When you're living on purpose, you don't feel the need to escape to the past or the future to find fulfillment. You can be fully content where you are. Even if you haven't achieved all your goals (yet), as long as you're following the trail of breadcrumbs and proactively incorporating your Purpose Triggers into your life, you will feel a profound sense of peace.

Along the same lines, when you're living on purpose, you are motivated by something greater than your ego, which is often disguised as the desire to prove something or achieve something. When you're aligned with your purpose—when you are truly lit up—you won't be as focused on a specific outcome or compare your progress to that of others. All that will matter is your ability to stay in your sweet spot and share your gifts with the world.

If you are committed to doing the work, you too will experience this peacefulness soon enough. You are exactly where you're meant to be. You picked up this book because you are *meant* to lead the way. Together, we have the potential to set a new standard—to encourage others to choose thriving over surviving. Your highlighted route will not be without detours or obstacles, but every one of these will sharpen your compass and give you greater confidence in your ability to stay the course. You are now equipped with a set of tools that can help you find your way back, no matter how far you stray. Use these tools wisely and share them freely with others.

It's time for you to take your new tricks for a spin in the real world. Fortunately, your internal GPS knows exactly where you're going and how to get there. Trust your inner voice and commit to showing up for yourself, for your life, and for those of us who are counting on you to live *on purpose*. Someone who set a powerful example in this regard is one of my favorite poets, Mary Oliver. She passed away at eighty-three in the same year I started writing this book. Growing up, Oliver was dirt poor, yet she chose to pursue writing, a profession that was notoriously trying and not exactly known as a cash cow. Her poetry celebrated nature as well as the real, raw human desires that we rarely feel comfortable admitting to—at least out loud. Perhaps her most famous poem, "Summer Day," highlights how something as seemingly small as curiosity can lead to something as grand as purpose. I want to leave you with the last two lines of this poem because they so beautifully encapsulate the challenge that I hope you are now ready to accept:

Tell me, what is it you plan to do
with your one wild and precious life?

# THE PURPOSE PLAYBOOK CHEAT SHEET

**Your purpose** = your sweet spot = your why.

**Your sweet spot** = where your passions, your strengths, and your potential to contribute intersect.

**Purpose Trigger** = an activity, person, environment, or feeling that gives you a heightened sense of meaning. A reminder of your why.

**Purpose Statement** = your sweet spot put into words.

**Living on purpose** = designing a life that allows you to operate in your sweet spot as often as possible by being intentional about incorporating your Purpose Triggers into your everyday. Living in wholehearted alignment with who you are *destined* to be, free from guilt, fear, or shame.

# *NOTES*

1        Howard Thurman, "The Sound of the Genuine: Spelman College Baccalaureate Address." May, 1980. The Howard Thurman and Sue Bailey Thurman Collections at Boston University. http://archives.bu.edu/web/howard-thurman/search/detail?id=352919

2        Bronnie Ware, "Regrets of the Dying." https://bronnieware.com/blog/regrets-of-the-dying/.

3        Kendall Cotton Bronka et al., "Purpose, Hope, and Life Satisfaction in Three Age Groups," *The Journal of Positive Psychology* 4, no. 6 (November 2009): 500–510.

4        Arelener D. Turner et al., "Is Purpose in Life Associated with Less Sleep Disturbance in Older Adults?" *Journal of Sleep Science and Practice* 1 (July 2017): Article 14.

5        Randy Cohen MD, MS et al. "Purpose in Life and Its Relationship to All Cause Mortality and Cardiovascular Events," *Journal of Psychosomatic Medicine* 78, no. 2 (February/March 2016): 122–133.

6        Andrew Steptoe and Daisy Fancourt, "Leading a Meaningful Life at Older Ages and its Relationship with Social

Engagement, Prosperity, Health, Biology, and Time Use," *Proceedings of the National Academy of Sciences in the United States of America* 116 (January 2019): 1207–1212. https://doi.org/10.1073/pnas.1814723116.


7      Dr. Gail Matthews, The Art and Science of Goal Setting study, *Dominican University of California.* 2015. https://www.dominican.edu/dominicannews/study-demonstrates-that-writing-goals-enhances-goal-achievement.


8      Roy F. Baumeister et al, "Bad is Stronger Than Good," *Review of General Psychology* 5, no. 4 (2001): 323–370.


9      See, for example, Courtney Ackerman, "83 Benefits of Journaling for Depression, Anxiety, and Stress," May 14, 2018. https://positivepsychologyprogram.com/benefits-of-journaling/.


10      J. M. Berg, J.E. Dutton, and A. Wrzesniewski, "What Is Job Crafting and Why Does It Matter?" retrieved June 22, 2009, from https://positiveorgs.bus.umich.edu/wp-content/uploads/What-is-Job-Crafting-and-Why-Does-it-Matter1.pdf.


11      J. M. Berg, J.E. Dutton, and A. Wrzesniewski, "Job Crafting and Meaningful Work," in *Purpose and Meaning in the Workplace,* ed. B. J. Dik, Z. S. Byrne, and M. F. Steger (Washington, DC: American Psychological Association, 2013), 81–104).


12      Ravi Mehta and Meng Zhu, "Creating When You Have Less: The Impact of Resource Scarcity on Product Use Creativity,"

*Journal of Consumer Research* 42, no. 5 (February 2016): 767–782, https://doi.org/10.1093/jcr/ucv051.

13      Allen R. Teo et al., "Social Relationships and Depression: Ten-Year Follow-Up from a Nationally Representative Study," *PLoS One*, 2013;8(4):e62396. doi:10.1371/journal.pone.006239.

14      Robert Waldinger, "What Makes a Good Life? Lessons from the Longest Study on Happiness," filmed November 2016 at TEDxBeaconStreet in Boston, MA. TED video, 12:40, https://www. ted.com/talks/robert_waldinger_what_makes_a_good_life_les-sons_from_the_longest_study_on_happiness.

15      Jennifer Wallace, "Why It's Good for Adults to Play," *Washington Post*, May 20, 2017. https://www.washingtonpost. com/national/health-science/why-its-good-for-grown-ups-to-go-play/2017/05/19/99810292-fd1f-11e6-8ebe-6e0dbe4f2bca_ story.html.

16      Lindsay Ashcraft. "5 Ways to Play like a Kid as an Adult," *Purpose Playbook* (blog). May 26, 2018. Accessed August 15, 2019. https://purposeplaybook.com/5-ways-to-play-like-a-kid-as-an-adult/.

17      Patrick L. Hill et al., "The Value of a Purposeful Life: Sense of Purpose Predicts Greater Income and Net Worth," *Journal of Research in Personality* 65 (December 2016): 38–42, https://doi. org/10.1016/j.jrp.2016.07.003.

# RECOMMENDED RESOURCES

## FREE DOWNLOADS

The Sweet Spot Finder
www.purposeplaybook.com/sweetspotfinder

The Purpose Statement Builder
www.purposeplaybook.com/statementbuilder

Purpose Trigger Alignment Exercise
www.purposeplaybook.com/alignmentplanner

The Purpose Planner
www.purposeplaybook.com/purposeplan

## PURPOSE READS

- *Deep Work: Rules for Focused Success in a Distracted World* by Cal Newport

- *When To Jump: If the Job You Have Isn't the Life You Want* by Mike Lewis

- *Daring Greatly: How the Courage to Be Vulnerable Transforms the Way We Live, Love, Parent, and Lead* by Brené Brown

- *Big Magic: Creative Living Beyond Fear* by Elizabeth Gilbert

- *You Are A Badass: How to Stop Doubting Your Greatness and Start Living an Awesome Life* by Jen Sincero

- *The Universe Has Your Back: Transform Fear to Faith* by Gabrielle Bernstein

- *Atomic Habits: An Easy & Proven Way to Build Good Habits & Break Bad Ones* by James Clear

- *Girl, Wash Your Face: Stop Believing the Lies About Who You Are So You Can Become Who You Were Meant to Be* by Rachel Hollis

- *The Power of Now: A Guide to Spiritual Enlightenment* by Eckhart Tolle

- *The Four Agreements: A Practical Guide to Personal Freedom* by Don Miguel Ruiz

- *Start With Why: How Great Leaders Inspire Everyone to Take Action* by Simon Sinek

- *The Alchemist* by Paolo Coelho

- *The Path Made Clear: Discovering Your Life's Direction and Purpose* by Oprah Winfrey

- *The Untethered Soul: The Journey Beyond Yourself* by Michael A. Singer

# *ACKNOWLEDGMENTS*

Like raising a child, writing a book takes a village. I want to acknowledge everyone who has contributed to this project—from those who read excerpts and shared feedback during my live workshops to those who expertly crafted the matcha lattes that fueled my writing process. And to everyone in between, THANK YOU.

A special thanks to:

- My family and family-in-law for your unconditional love and support. In particular, my dad, Evert, for giving me permission to spread my wings and always providing a safe space to land. I will be forever grateful.

- My husband, Jeff, for believing in me and for pushing me to never (ever) settle. You not only make me a better writer, you make me a better person.

- My cofounder, Nellie, for embracing my crazy passion projects. *The Purpose Playbook* would not exist without you.

- The Morris family, for allowing me to honor the legendary Daddy Mac.

- My beta readers, Stephanie, Abbie, Jeanneke, Roy, and Ryan, for giving me invaluable feedback and encouragement when I needed it most.

- All the authors, leaders, and legends mentioned in this book for inspiring me with your extraordinary insights and achievements.

- The team at Wise Ink and my editor, Kristen Tate, for investing in this project and making my first foray into publishing such an enjoyable experience.

# SPEAKING AND WORKSHOPS

From business conferences and college campuses to intimate board rooms and retreats, Alexandra can help audiences of all ages and sizes overcome common roadblocks and make meaningful progress towards designing their lives around what matters most.

Each speaking engagement is tailored to the audience and the objective. Alexandra incorporates jaw-dropping insights, relatable anecdotes, and interactive exercises to deliver an engaging experience that seeks to inspire and empower. With an emphasis on action, Alexandra is focused on sharing tactical tips and tools to help her audience transform their lives, teams, and companies.

If you're interested in booking Alexandra Cole for an upcoming event, conference, or retreat, please visit www.PurposePlaybook.com/speaking or send an inquiry to hello@alexandracole.com.

# ABOUT THE AUTHOR

Alexandra Cole is the cofounder of Purpose Generation, a millennial insights and strategy firm that helps iconic Fortune 500 brands better understand and engage the next generation of consumers and talent. In 2016, Alexandra created the Find Your Purpose workshop to provide a practical, no-nonsense roadmap to living a more purpose-filled life. She has facilitated the workshop at businesses, schools, co-working spaces, and retreats across the world, and built a coaching practice around her methodology. Along the way, she discovered that what connects all generations—at work and beyond—is a deep desire to find more fulfillment in their every day.

Alexandra started her career at Bain & Company in New York. She was born in London, raised in the Netherlands, educated at Princeton University, and currently lives in Santa Barbara, California with her husband. She is insatiably curious when it comes to people and what motivates them. She is happiest when writing, engaged in good conversation, exploring new places, or on her yoga mat. Alexandra's work has appeared in the *Huffington Post* and on Forbes.com. *The Purpose Playbook* is her first book.